WHO ARE WE? RELIGIOUS, PHILOSOPHICAL, SCIENTIFIC, AND TRANSHUMANIST THEORIES OF HUMAN NATURE

John G. Messerly, PhD

Dedication

To Jane, who has a beautiful nature.

Contents

Preface

Without knowing what I am and why I am here, life is impossible.
~ Leo Tolstoy

Insignificant mortals, who are as leaves are,
and now flourish and grow warm with life,
and feed on what the ground gives,
but then again fade away and are dead. ~ Homer

[Human are] still embryonic ... [human are] the bud from which
something more complicated and more centered than [humans
themselves] should emerge. ~ Pierre Teilhard de Chardin

All my life I struggled to stretch my mind to the breaking point,
until it began to creak, in order to create a great thought which
might be able to give a new meaning to life, a new meaning to
death, and to console mankind. ~ Nikos Kazantzakis

The **first** part of this book asks the question: *Who are we?* We
may think we know the answer to this question, but there are
possibilities we haven't considered. For example, we may think
that what we are is inside our bodies, but perhaps that's wrong.
Why do we end where our bodies do? After all, our skin is porous
and interacts with the environment. We can't survive for more than
a few minutes without the air, so why isn't the air as much a part of
us as our lungs or legs? And for us there is no breathable air
without plants, so why aren't they a part of us too? In fact, our
existence depends on the earth's ecosystem and the sun. Following
this line of thinking, our existence ultimately depends on the entire
universe.

So perhaps we aren't egos inside bags of skin; perhaps we aren't
separate egos at all. Maybe we are like windows, apertures or
vortexes through which the universe is conscious of itself for a

i

brief moment. While we are fond of saying things like "I came into this world," as if our essence was preparing to wage war on reality isn't it more accurate to say, "I came out of the universe?" Don't people come out of the universe like leaves come out of trees, or waves come out of oceans?

And such questions are not merely academic. If we feel separate from the world, then it is alien to us; it becomes something we must *confront*. But if we see that are connected the universe, then we are more likely to treat it as our home. We will realize that the environment that surrounds our bodies is as much a part of us as our heart or lungs. If we despoil the environment, we despoil ourselves; if we destroy the environment, we destroy ourselves. So perhaps we are the universe looking at itself from billions of perspectives. In fact, couldn't we say that we *are* the universe slowly becoming self-conscious?

These are just some of the ideas we will consider in this book. What we will discover is that there are many ways of thinking about human nature. We might be mostly social selves as Confucius thought, or God in disguise like Shankara believed, or have no self like the Buddha claimed. Aristotle and Kant thought we are primarily rational creatures, but Marx and Freud believed that we are largely determined by societal or irrational influences, while Sartre argued that the only nature we have is the one we create. But one thing is certain, we are animals with a long evolutionary history, and we will continue to evolve as science and technology transform us. We now know where we came from, but we are not sure where are we going.

In discussing individual theories of I will consider each theory as encompassing a: 1) theory of reality; 2) theory of human nature; 3) major problem of life; and 4) solution to that problem. I hope that this will both better explain the theories, and allow them to be compared with each other.

We will begin by examining various religious systems that originated in the axial age: Confucianism, Hinduism, Buddhism, and Judeo-Christianity. Then, we will discuss the philosophical theories of Plato, Aristotle, Epicurus, Kant and Sartre, as well as two theories of human nature from the social scientists Marx and Freud. Next we will turn to Darwin and the neo-Darwinians for insights into human nature from evolutionary biology. Finally, we will ponder the future of human nature, especially how science and technology will transform human nature to the extent that we may become post-human.

Generally early theories of human nature are religious, modern theories of our nature respond to science or are full-fledged scientific theories, and theories about the future consider how science and technology will transform our nature. This transition from religious descriptions of reality and human nature to scientific ones is not surprising, given the rise of influence of science since the seventeenth-century. Today science is the only cognitive authority in the world, and if we really want to know who we are we must understand something of modern science, particularly our evolutionary history. And once we take an evolutionary perspective we will see that our descendents, should they survive, will come to resemble us about as much as we do the amino acids from which we sprang.

Such concerns lead to the **second** part of our book which asks: *what is the future of human nature?* Here we will consider technologies like robotics, artificial intelligence, genetic engineering and nanotechnology may transform human nature, including *defeating death* itself. If some of these things come to pass surely we will move from human to post-human.

Consideration of the future leads us to the **third** part of our book which asks: *what is the meaning of life?* We will try to understand the question and a number of answers that have been proposed by religion, philosophy, and science. Then we will be bold enough to suggest our own answer to this question.

This book has its origins in university classes in "Philosophy of Human Nature" and "Philosophy of the Human Person" that I taught for almost thirty years. In those classes I used various editions of a book by Leslie Stevenson called *Twelve Theories of Human Nature*. It was a great textbook, and my book began as notes summarizing the Stevenson book for my students. In fact, the first third of this book still summarizes much of the Stevenson book, and I encourage readers who want more detail about those theories of human nature to consult that book. But I wanted to write a book with less detail and more breadth, and one which included an in-depth discussion of the future of human nature as well as the meaning of life. This is that book.

Chapter 1 – Religious Theories of Human Nature

Confucianism: Humans Are Social Beings

Theory of Reality

Confucius (551 – 479 BCE) cared about human beings and the human condition—not about metaphysics or grand theories of the universe. Worry about humans, not gods; worry about life, not death, he said. He emphasized that good government promotes social harmony and the general well-being. Thus Confucius is primarily a political thinker.

One of the few metaphysical components to his thought is his view that morality is embedded in the universe, as well as in human beings. For Confucius, the just person cares about the general welfare, and rulers who rule for their own benefit rather than the general welfare will not be supported by what Confucius called the *decree of heaven*. But while it is nice to think that the heavens favor the just, it is hard to believe this when we look around the world. Could it be, contrary to Confucian thinking, that the heavens support selfish leaders?

The other metaphysical concept in Confucian thinking is the idea that some things are beyond our control—the result of destiny. Confucius talked as if destiny is a design of heaven that is beyond human understanding. The decree of Heaven refers to the natural order of things, but it's not clear what he means by the heavens, except that it's not a supernatural concept. Humans can conform to the decree of heaven—by promoting the general welfare—but our destiny is beyond our understanding and control. Humans should

1

follow the decree of heaven by being unconcerned with wealth, status, longevity, etc.

Human Nature

Confucius was optimistic about human potential; he wanted people to be sages who instantiate the goodness of the heavens by being benevolent. When you read this beautiful idea it's hard not to contrast it with all the ugliness that surrounds us, but Confucius himself remained hopeful. He thought that benevolence led to happiness, a theme later echoed by Socrates, Plato, and Aristotle. Still Confucius recognized that most people are not sages, they are miserable. But why?

Confucius was not clear as to why so few people become wise, benevolent sages, but he suggested that we might freely choose not to be good. He also thought that environment plays a large role in shaping us, and that that we need to be molded by culture in order to achieve moral perfection. So he saw clearly the tension between freedom and determinism, a classic philosophical problem.

The Problem

Selfishness and ignorance of the past cause social discord, human life is marred by discontent, corruption, injustice, greed, and the like. But why is life so bad? Confucius responded that life is bad because of: 1) profit motive; 2) lack of respect for parents; 3) lying; 4) ignorance of the past; 5) little benevolence.

1. Morality and profit stand in opposition; the wise understand justice, the small person understands profit. Most are guided by self-interest, especially in wealth or profit. This leads to immoral results and social disharmony.

2. Selfishness motivated by profit implies a lack of respect for others including other family members. If you don't act ethically within the family, you will spread your discord throughout society.

3. People lie. So it is better to recognize that actions speak louder than words. If there is no connection between actions and words there is no basis for societal trust.

4. Without knowledge of past sages, people have no moral insight. In other words moral education is important.

5. The most important virtue is benevolence, which is moral perfection. Yet Confucius realized this virtue is rare, hence life is filled with strife.

The Solution

Confucius prescribed self-discipline for individuals and rulers in order to cure the ills of society. In other words, society will be better when the people who make it up are more moral. This approach provides answers to the five problems listed above.

1. Profit - Do what is right because it is *right*, not for profit. By struggling to be moral Confucius thought we align ourselves with the decree of heaven. We also shield ourselves against disappointment when we care about moral virtue rather than with things we can't be assured of getting—like fame and fortune. Moral excellence, he thought, is its own reward. If we are motivated by what is right, we will find joy in our efforts even if we don't fully succeed. While destiny plays a role in human life, moral excellence is within our control and it can be attained through self-

3

discipline. Thus, we should cultivate self, not social recognition, fame or fortune.

2. Parents - Cultivating self implies you will be a better family member. This emphasis on the community rather than the individual stands in marked contrast with the prescriptions of Western culture. Confucius was less interested in individualism, since being a good member of the community and family reverberates through society in positive ways. A person who is good to their parents, siblings and children will be good to others as well. Transformation of the self and benevolence begin in the family and spread outward. Confucius suggests that we should follow the ways of our parents, if they were virtuous. This may sound strange to our individualistic ears, but the idea is that we learn from those who have gone before us.

3. Lying - Confucius said we need word and deed to conform—actions should reflect words. If we all lie, trust will evaporate. Think how communication would fall apart if you couldn't ordinarily assume people were telling the truth. Why ask for the time or directions if people usually lie? If we use words to conceal the truth, social chaos ensues. Trust is crucial to society.

4. History - The answer to ignorance of the past is education. For Confucius, the study of our cultural legacy reveals how moral perfection may be achieved. Such education is also crucial for good government. (China took these ideas seriously. For more than a thousand years demonstrating mastery of Confucian texts by passing the Imperial exams was a prerequisite to hold political office. The historian Will

Durant argues that this resulted in the best government in history. The philosopher Voltaire and others have also praised the system.)

5. Benevolence - Kindness, charity, and compassion are the means of attaining moral perfection. The process of becoming benevolent involved three elements: a) clinging to benevolence at all times; b) treating others as you would like to be treated and not doing to others what you don't want done to you; and c) habitually acting according to moral rules, which we learn from studying the classics. So we achieve benevolence by acting in accord with the moral rules we learn by studying, which is to live according to the way of the heavens.

This goal of attaining self-discipline, self-mastery, or self-perfection takes a lifetime. Benevolence is the outward expression of this internal state, and serves as a model to others who want to be sages. For the sages benevolent action naturally flows from their character; it's the expression of their internal perfected state. The self-disciplined person models their behavior on the behavior of the sages, with the goal of becoming sages themselves. Hence moral perfection is a process of development. As Confucius says, the master and student may appear similar from the outside, but unlike the student, the master does things naturally and spontaneously. In the end we achieve moral perfection by studying the classics and becoming a sage. If people bettered themselves, society would improve. I think Confucius would agree with Spinoza, a Dutch philosopher, who centuries later would right:

> How would it be possible, if salvation were ready to our hand, and could without great labour be found, that it should be by almost all men neglected? But all things excellent are as difficult as they are rare.

Chapter 1 – Religious Theories of Human Nature

Mencius and Hsun-tzu

But is human nature originally good or evil? Two subsequent Confucian philosophers discussed this issue. Mencius subscribed to the former view, while Hsun-tzu to the latter.

Mencius thought that people are naturally drawn to good things like compassion, benevolence, dutifulness and wisdom. Still Mencius granted that people are also selfish, and the good qualities of the human heart must be cultivated to help people be virtuous. If we receive parental love, a good education, societal support, and our basic needs are met, then we have an excellent chance of being wise and just people. Mencius even offered an argument that humans are inherently good: if we see a child in danger most of us would instinctively try to help.

Hsun-tzu argued that unlimited desires dominate our interior life and, as resources are limited, conflict between people results. So our nature is generally bad, and we must work consciously to be good. This is all reminiscent of Hobbes' argument that the state of nature is a state of war precisely because the things we want—fame, fortune, etc.—are in short supply. Hsun-tzu also says that the desire for profit, as well as envy and hatred are the natural tendencies which lead to strife, violence, crime, and wantonness. Still he believed that with proper education, moral excellence can be achieved, although this takes effort and must be aided by a good culture.

Thus, despite their disagreements, both Mencius and Hsun-tzu agreed that the path of sagehood consists of action based on the examples of past sages. For Hsun-tzu we are naturally warped boards that need to be straightened; for Mencius we are relatively straight boards that can be warped. But no matter what our human nature, Confucianism affirms that wise and just people will create good societies.

Hinduism: Humans Are Divine

Theory of Reality

Hinduism, like any religion, is diverse, and we can't capture that diversity in a few pages. So to introduce ourselves to it, we will focus on the Upanishads, the most foundational texts of Hinduism. According to the Upanishads, all reality is *one*. This ultimate reality is called Brahman, a force, power, or energy that pervades everything. Ultimately, all of reality is one; all is Brahman.

But why then does reality appear to be composed of many things like stars, trees, rocks and chairs? A possible answer lies in the Hindu creation myth. All originates in nothingness except for Brahman. Being lonely Brahman divided into female and male, and from this the entire plurality of the elements of the universe came into being. However, the original unity never disappears; it just takes on the appearance of multiplicity. So again multiplicity is ultimately an illusion—there is really only Brahman.

This also implies that Braham is both immanent and transcendent—it both within and outside all reality. This view is called panentheism, the view that the divine interpenetrates all of nature and timelessly extends beyond it. These are the two aspects of Brahman. It is both all the changing things of the world, as well as the unchanging ground of all things. This is the one ultimate reality seen from different perspectives. But in the end there is only Brahman. Finally, there is a tension in Hinduism between those who believe Brahman is ineffable and impossible to conceptualize, and those who disagree, identifying Brahman with everything.

Human Nature

We are all one and thus radically interconnected with all being. The self or soul within all, the *Atman*, is connected (identical?) with all other selves. We are all like spokes connected to a central

7

hub or, more radically, we are identical with all reality. Hinduism distinguishes the transitory self as ego or I with the eternal, immortal self, the Atman. This true self is identical with Brahman. In short, you are God.

Atman is not an object of consciousness; it is consciousness itself and thus can't be known like other objects. Our true selves are identical with the consciousness which animates all consciousness. We are not transient egos inside bodies, but ultimately identical with all reality. Again *Atman is Brahman*. You are identical with whatever power, force or energy animates all reality; you are (non-personal) god.

And this true self migrates from body to body. To make reincarnation plausible to modern ears, consider that people die and other people are born, in other words Atman/Brahman continues. Remember though that this is a brief, general description of Hinduism; there is a lot of disagreement in Hinduism as in other religions. For example some believe in Saguna Brahman, a personal god with attributes; others believe in Nirguna Brahman, a transpersonal god without attributes. Some Hindus defend non-dualism; others defend dualism.

The Problem

The main problem of human existence is *ignorance* regarding the nature of ultimate reality. Most don't recognize the reality of infinite Brahman, and thus identify with the transitory objects of consciousness. Thus ignorance of the fact that Atman is Brahman is ultimately ignorance of our true selves. When we identify with the phenomenal world instead of with Brahman, we display our ignorance. We concern ourselves with our little egos and threats of offenses to them, rather than recognizing our egos as illusory. As a result we are alienated from ourselves, from others, and from all reality. We are isolated and lonely.

This misguided individualism is caused by karma, a moral law of cause and effect. This means that our actions aren't free, but determined by past desires and actions. We are in psychological bondage to previous actions and the desires that caused them. Hindu meditation in large part is an attempt to get in touch with our true nature and free us from egoistic desires.

The Solution

Hinduism is generally optimistic about attaining freedom from desire, and the discovery of our true nature. We attain freedom and self-discovery through: a) knowledge; b) love; c) work; or d) psychological exercises. The path we choose depends in large part on our personality. More intellectual types might realize their unity with reality through knowledge; more emotional types might realize this through love; more active types through work. And meditation is good for everyone. But the goal is the same—to come to know that you are nothing more and nothing less than the power, force, or energy that animates all of reality. You are God.

Shankara's Non-Dualism

The two most important interpreters of Hinduism are Shankara (788 -820) and Ramanuja (? – 1137)

Shankara asked how Brahman relates to the world as it appears to our senses. His is a philosophy of total unity. For Shankara, Brahman is the only reality and is without attribute, while the world is unreal and distinctions between Brahman and the individual are illusory. To fully realize Brahman, all distinctions between subjects and objects fade away, since there is only one reality.

Shankara concluded that the phenomenal world is maya; it is illusory. *Maya* is the process through which we perceive multiplicity, even though reality is one. The world as it appears to our senses is not Brahman, and thus not ultimately real. This does not mean the world is imaginary—it is real—but it is not ultimate or absolute reality. It is derivative of Brahman. The world of the senses exists in relation to Brahman the way a dream stands in relation to being awake. We may think that a rope in dim light is a snake, even though in good light we can tell the difference. By analogy, the world of multiplicity is superimposed on Brahman, similar to the way the snake might is superimposed on the rope. When we realize our unity with Brahman, we will experience the world as less real.

For Shankara, the idea of a *personal god* (Saguna Brahman) with attributes is ultimately an illusion, since Brahman isn't limited by attributes. Personal gods play a role for those enmeshed in the illusion of maya, the notion of a personal god who you can talk to helps people reject the attachments of this world. But ultimately (Nirguna) Brahman is transpersonal, and without attributes.

And Shankara also rejects the *individual soul*. Positing an individual soul is better than being attached to one's ego and body, but the final realization is that the true self is Atman or pure consciousness. Thus the world, god, and the individual soul are mere appearances—the ultimate and only reality is Brahman. *Atman is Brahman*. This is the ultimate realization in Hinduism; it is the goal of spirituality. There is no ultimate distinction between subjects and objects, for there are no multiplicities that can be distinguished. We are like drops of water trying to understand that we are ultimately united in one big ocean of being.

A necessary step in this spiritual journey is the realization that desire, especially for the things and activities of this world, must be eradicated. The highest spiritual path consists of renunciation of the world followed by a lifetime of meditation designed to confirm the insight that you are Brahman.

Ramanuja's Dualism

For Ramanuja the divine is personal, and multiplicity is real. Brahman is still the sole reality, but with different aspects or qualities. Ramanuja accepts a personal god—a god with personality and qualities. The love of god entails a subject knowing and loving an object. Ramanuja wants to taste sugar not be sugar.

And the physical world is real for Ramanuja. It was created from divine love. It's the transformation of Brahman, similar to the way that milk transforms into cheese. In this view the world isn't something to be overcome but something to be appreciated as the product of Brahman's creativity. Maya refers not to illusion, but to this creative process. Thus the world is god's body. The world is an attribute of the eternal god analogous to the idea that the body is an attribute of the soul. The soul is part of god, but it is both different and not different from god. This "paradoxical logic" can be hard for Westerners to understand, but the idea is that truth is paradoxical. The soul separates from Brahman at creation, and returns to Brahman at dissolution. Yet the soul is still somehow both separate and eternal.

The path to freedom for Ramanuja consists of action that is unattached to results. We will be more effective if we are not overly concerned with the results of our actions. After all, the world is *Lila*, or god's play, and we are the actors not the playwright. We need not renounce the world, but revel in it. As for worshipping various manifestations of the gods, Ramanuja believed this helps most people. The goal of these devotional acts is a feeling of the presence of gods, not oneness with a god. The majority of Hindus practice in this way. Something similar could be said about almost all religious traditions, they emphasize the emotional and devotional rather than the abstract and intellectual.

11

Buddhism: Humans Have No Self

The Buddha's Life and Thought

The story of the Buddha, independent of its historicity, is crucial to understanding Buddhism. Siddhartha Gautama was born a privileged prince after a miraculous birth—by legend a white elephant entered his mother's womb through her side. Siddhartha grew up as a young prince shielded from life's unpleasantness until, while riding outside the palace one day, he saw: old age, sickness, death, and a monk who had renounced the world. Buddha thought the monk revealed a possible way out of suffering and, in response he left his wife, newborn son, and the comfort of the palace.

For the next six years he tried ascetic experiences with no success—nearly starving to death in the process. Eventually he found a middle way between the opulent decadence of palace life and extreme asceticism. While sitting under the Bodhi tree, determined not to leave until he achieved enlightenment, he finally attained *enlightenment.* Siddhartha Gautama had become the Buddha, the Awakened One. He decided to share his insights with others, and his own life became the model for the monastic life of a Buddhist monk. He died, surrounded by his followers at the age of eighty.

To understand Buddhism, consider this. When confronted with the great questions, the Buddha refused to answer them, insisting that the religious life doesn't depend on dogma. One will die before these questions are answered. Buddha likened asking metaphysical questions with claiming—after being struck by a poison arrow—that you won't have the arrow removed until you know who wounded you, what kind of person they were, the nature of the arrow, etc. Again, such a person would die before all their questions are answered.

Moreover even if you had answers to all these abstract questions what good would it do? Would you cease to suffer in this life? Buddha didn't think so, arguing that eliminating suffering is paramount. So Buddhism is anti-metaphysical. It doesn't construct esoteric theories, but seeks to understand the nature, causes, origins, and the removal of suffering. Buddhism is like medicine that we use until we gain full health.

Theory of Reality

The three fundamental characteristics of existence for the Buddha are:

1. radical impermanence (constant change);

2. lack of a solid self (no self);

3. unsatisfactoriness (suffering).

The *first* mark of existence captures life's transitory, ephemeral, fleeting nature. Nothing in the world is solid or independent of anything else. And nothing—no idea, being, state of mind or thing—endures. Everything is impermanent, changing constantly at every moment. Moreover, everything is dependent upon and interconnected with other things, without which we wouldn't exist— our lives are contingent upon the existence of our parents, grandparents, gravity, evolution, air, water, and the sun and stars.

Consider also how our thoughts and desires, our loves and hates, are largely out of our control. Consider also how much mental suffering we endure on this basis. Buddhism aims to free us from the ignorance that is at the root of all this suffering. Of course our present life is one in a long series, and our present condition is determined by past actions. Karma denotes this moral law of cause and effect. To make this scientifically believable consider how many of your behaviors emanate from your biological past, or your social and cultural heritage. This karma is enough to propel the universe along in Buddhism, there are no creator or sustainer gods. Generally there are no personal gods in Buddhism.

Human Nature

The *second* mark of existence is that there is nothing solid or permanent about the self. There is no self, or no atman.   To understand this, consider the car you drive, or the university you attend. They are both made up of many parts, and the word car or university applies to all of the parts that make up the car or university. But the car or university doesn't have a soul or essence over and above those parts and their relationships. A car or university is simply all its parts and the relationship between those parts. Similarly, you are the sum of your parts and their interrelationships; there is no separate soul or essence to you anymore than there is to your car or university. Buddhists claim to confirm this truth in meditation, and it is one of the most fascinating ideas I've encountered in my philosophical career.

Of course you do have some continuity of memory, but there is nothing permanent underlying your being. You are a mind, body, and stream of consciousness. You aren't really a being at all (a substance), but a becoming (an event.) The idea that you are a separate ego is also harmful because it leads to fear of death, violence, theft, and completion. Realizing the self as illusory leads to compassion—the most important Buddhist virtue.

The idea of the separate ego is an expression of the five attachments or components (skandas) that make up what we call a person. These components are:

1. form—the body and its sense organs;

2. sensations—the physiological process produced by the contact of senses and the world;

3. perception—sensations that lead to object recognition;

4. mental formations—our predispositions, attitudes, tendencies, habits, and;

5. consciousness—we sense and perceive, we become aware of things; consciousness is awareness.

Perhaps the most important components are the mental formations, which themselves result from the interplay of bodies, sensations, perceptions, and conscious awareness. All of this leaves karmic residue in our minds. But how do we form mental constructs? And how much reality depends on consciousness? The Buddhists believe that our consciousness is conditioned, almost determined, by our mental formations. Previous experience conditions our consciousness, perhaps forever.

Consciousness consists of these ever changing states of mind. Like a chariot that exists momentarily on a single point of its wheels, we live only for a brief moment of a single thought. We are changing every millisecond. There is nothing permanent about us, not even for a moment. You may think that pieces of bronze or iron are stable, but they too change slowly every moment. Just visit ancient ruins to confirm this. Everything is radically impermanent. Ask yourself this. Are you the same or different than when you were six years old? In one sense you are the same—born of the same parents, same DNA—but in another sense you are radically different. You have been in a constant state of flux.

The Buddhists explain the self using a candle flame. At every moment it is different—you are always changing—but there is a connection between the candle flame now and the flame an hour ago—you have some psychological continuity with your six year old self. How then do we explain reincarnation? The Buddhists explain this with an analogy—it is like one candle relighting another new one as the old one burns out. (This reminds me of the philosopher Lucretius, who said we are like runners who hand the flame of life one unto another.)

Still, despite the orthodoxy, the Buddha himself refused to answer the question of whether a separate, permanent soul exists. I respect his hesitancy to answer such deep questions, no doubt he thought they distracted us from the problem of suffering. I first encountered Buddhism forty years ago and, with each new encounter, I am always moved by its profundity.

The Problem

We begin with the *four noble truths*. The *first* noble truth is that life is full of *suffering* and dissatisfaction. (This is also the third mark of existence.) We suffer from anxiety, insecurity, uncertainty, fear, frustration, disappointment and loss—everything is imperfect and flawed. The first kind of suffering is ordinary suffering: aging, sickness, death, unpleasant conditions, sadness, pain, not getting what we want, etc. The second kind results from change, even happiness is fleeting and ephemeral. The last type of suffering results from a false sense of ego. We suffer when slighted, insulted, not recognized, etc. The Buddha doesn't say that life is essentially or only suffering, but that we experience a lot of it. This is not meant to be pessimistic, but realistic—dissatisfaction is the basic problem of life.

The *second* noble truth identifies the cause of suffering as *craving*, grasping, desiring. We want money, sex, power, drugs, food, fame, etc. What happens? When in the state of wanting, we are dissatisfied. Then we get what we want, but soon want more.

16

Who Are We?

We want a thousand dollars and then a million and then a billion—and we are still unhappy. The thrill of the new car or house makes us happy for a short time, but not for long. In fact, studies show that after we have an income to fulfill our basic needs more money doesn't make us happier. Does a glass of wine taste good? Maybe. Do ten glasses make you feel better? Not likely. Is it nice to have a roof over your head? Yes. Does having ten houses make your happier? Not likely. This is what Buddha is getting at when he says our desires cause our troubles.

The Solution

The end of craving and desiring is the key to relieving suffering. This is the *third* noble truth. This leads to the state of nirvana, a peaceful state without desire. But what do we do to achieve this blissful state? We understand the *fourth* noble truth, which is to follow the *eightfold path*, also known as the Middle Way between a life of complete asceticism and a life of desiring pleasure. This path addresses ethical conduct, which is based on compassion; mental discipline, which flows from meditative practice and leads to the realization of the true nature of self; and wisdom, which is the realization of the true nature of reality.

Ethical components of the eightfold path include: 1) *right speech*—speech that tries to benefit others, speech that doesn't lie, and silence when called for; 2) *right action*—moral, honorable, and peaceful conduct, no lying, killing, cheating, stealing, and the like; and 3) *right livelihood*—making a living without harming others.

Mental discipline is comprised of: 4) *right effort*—working toward wholesome rather than unwholesome states of mind; 5) *right mindfulness*—achieved through mindfulness meditation that leads to a better understanding of the impermanent nature of reality and lack of self; and 6) *right concentration*—meditation on a single point like the breath, a flame, an image, or a mantra.

Wisdom includes: 7) *right thought*—detachment from the idea of self; and 8) *right understanding*—accepting the three marks of existence (life is impermanent, there is no self, and there is suffering), and harmonizing the mind with this realization. It also implies accepting the four noble truths.

Theravada and Mahayana

For monks this involves selfless, detached actions which aim to free one from karmic residue, ultimately leading to enlightenment. For the laity this involves doing good deeds, accepting the five precepts—don't kill, steal, lie, consume intoxicant or have illicit sex—and improving their karmic lot. The monks provide a model of the spiritual life; the laity provides minimal food for the monks. In the Theravadan tradition the monk who reaches nirvana is the ideal, while in the Mahayana tradition the bodhisattva does not enter nirvana but stays in this world helping the rest of us be liberated. In some schools of the Mahayana tradition the idea our true consciousness already exists within us, and we must work to uncover it. In short, the Mahayana tradition recognizes other ways besides the monastic life to enlightenment, including devotional practices.

Judeo-Christianity: Humans Are God's Servants

Part I: The Old Testament

The Old Testament is recognized as the word of god by both Jews and Christians; the New Testament is only recognized as such by Christians. Islam also recognizes the patriarchs and prophets of these books, but asserts that Muhammad is the last and greatest of the prophets, and the Koran is Allah's unique message. While

Judeo-Christianity is varied—there are more than 41,000 denomination of Christianity in the world today—we will begin with a theory of reality common to both Jews and Christians.

Theory of Reality

It's not clear from the opening verses of the Bible whether god is one (monotheism) or many (polytheism.) There are also other well-known conundrums. For example, there are two creation accounts corresponding to the first two chapters of the book. In the first, humans were created after the animals, and man and woman were created simultaneously; in the second, humans were created before animals, with man created first, then the animals and then a woman from man's rib. The god in these stories creates by commanding, and all creation is good. Soon the first two humans disobey god, then one of their children kills the other, and god resolves to kill all humans. Finally, Noah is allowed to save his family and all the animals. There are also stories of sons of god having sex with woman and races of giants. No doubt the text is a compilation of multiple ancient stories.

The god of the Bible speaks to people, instructs them, and is represented variously as having a face and voice, being a shield, having nostrils, being a shepherd, and more. In later books he generally speaks through intermediaries, and later on still there is less talk of god. So how do we distinguish the symbolic, metaphorical talk about God from realistic, literal talk of God? There is a lot to say here, but most Biblical scholars believe the creation story is a myth, and its talk of god metaphorical.

Human Nature

Humans have a relationship to god, who has created them in a special place in the universe. Is this to be taken literally or mythologically? The accounts can't be taken literally because there are multiple and contradictory creation stories. Also the stories are inconsistent with modern science, including but not limited to cosmology, geology, and biology. Science provides entirely different accounts of our past. Moreover, these stories contradict common sense. How did Adam and Eve's sons find wives if all humans were descended from the first couple? Frankly, a serious informed reader can't take these stories literally, they are myths.

God supposedly made humans in his image. Humans are thus special, yet also continuous with nature. But in the Old Testament view, humans aren't made up of body and soul. The Hebrew word *ruach* means wind or breath; it is not a separate soul. The idea of a disembodied soul isn't found anywhere in the Hebrew Bible. In fact, there is no expectation of the afterlife in the Old Testament; the Jews develop the idea of the afterlife only slightly before the time of Jesus. This is one of the most common misunderstandings of orthodox Christianity by Christians—one doesn't die and go to the afterlife. Just read St. Paul if you doubt this.

As for woman, the one biblical account has them appearing second to man. Women bring about man's fall and tempt him to sin, especially sexual sin. For their disobedience woman will suffer in childbirth and must accept men as their masters. Of course god is a man and most of this was written by men. Why aren't we surprised by this?

Humans can accept or reject their god, although there is a tension here because woman supposedly should submit to men. God commanded humans not to learn about good and evil—to eat from the tree of the knowledge of good and evil—and their eternal salvation depends on not doing this. But why is it bad to learn this? Isn't it a mark of maturity to put childhood behind and search for our own answers? Here we confront the emphasis on faith characteristic of the Hebraic mind, which will contrast strikingly with the Hellenistic (Greek) emphasis on reason.

The emphasis on faith implies a concern with good actions and personal traits. But faith in the godhead is of primary importance, we were created to love and serve god. We should obey our god. That's why god rewards Abraham because he is willing to kill his own son Isaac in order to submit to god. Kierkegaard famously called Abraham the "knight of faith" for doing this, although we might call Abraham insane and god malicious for their participation. What kind of god would play such a trick on someone? Another example of the emphasis on faith versus reason issue is in the story of Job. Satan persuades god to torment Job for no reason. God asserts his authority and Job submits. The point seems to be that one should be humble before god, rather than there being any intellectual insight as to why this has all happened to Job.

The Problem

We misuse our freedom, and choose evil over good which severs our relationship with god. God punishes our disobedience by sending pain, suffering, and death. Thus, there is a tension between our inclinations and our duties.

The Solution

God made us to be in a relationship with him, we broke that relationship, so god must fix it—hence the idea of salvation initiated by the mercy of god. In the Old Testament this is described as the idea of a covenant between god and his chosen people—the Jews. Still problems persist, sin doesn't disappear from the earth, the Jews commit genocide that god orders, and more. God uses history to punish both friends and foes alike, but the idea arises that god's mercy will intervene in history to rectify all these problems. Thus the Jews began to hope that God would send a savior, which Christians identify as Jesus.

Part II: The New Testament

The Jewish rabbi Jesus didn't leave any writing, and the new religion of Christianity developed with the letters of St. Paul and the gospel narratives about his life written between forty to seventy years after his death. Of course this assumes that Jesus was a historical figure, a claim that some scholars doubt.

Theory of Reality

Christians soon recognized god the father, god the son, and god the holy spirit who inspire Christian believers—three persons in one god. What is a Christian? At a minimum it requires believing that Jesus was a special, historical, revelation of god, and that god was uniquely present in Jesus. This is expressed as the doctrine of the incarnation—Jesus is both human and divine. What this doctrine means is a matter of theological dispute. However, the issue was settled historically for Christians at the Council of Nicaea in 325 in a debate among council members. Jesus was a hybrid god-man.

Human Nature

St. Paul talks of both spirit and flesh. Paul praised the former and denigrated the latter. The idea, later expressed in the Sermon on the Mount, seems to be that the best of human nature rejects power, fame, wealth, and sex for moral righteousness. Sex is a particularly vexing, as both St. Paul and St. Augustine deride it. As for women, Jesus evidently didn't choose any as disciples, and St. Paul and Christianity have found women theologically problematic ever since.

Paul doesn't seem to believe in an afterlife, although some have obviously interpreted the Kingdom of God in this way. However, the New Testament does discuss the resurrection, last judgment, and eternal punishment. The idea that Jesus was resurrected has traditionally been taken to imply that we can live forever too, at least if we are saved by god. The Christian expectation of resurrection of the saved appears in Corinthians.

The Problem and the Solution

The problem is that we are all imperfect in god's eyes, since human beings rejected god by eating the forbidden fruit. How then are we to be saved? While it is unclear what Jesus thought of himself, it was Paul who first formulized the doctrines of salvation and the incarnation. Paul thought that god is uniquely present in Jesus, and somehow Jesus' life, death, and resurrection restore our relationship with god. Paul believed that one misdeed condemned all humanity and one righteous act—Jesus dying—saves everyone. This is the solution to the problem of separation from God.

But it's counter-intuitive to believe that one bad act and one good act could do this. And how does Jesus atone for our sins anyway? Today most theologians don't accept the idea that this was a blood sacrifice like in the Old Testament. So again, how does this supposed event two thousand years ago redeem the world of sin? Traditionally we are saved by god's grace, not our own works. Yet Christianity assumes we are free to choose to accept god's salvation. This creates a tension. These are problems for Christian theologians to try to resolve.

Chapter 2 – Philosophical Theories of Human Nature

Plato: Humans Are Multi-Faceted

Plato's Life and Works

At the time of Plato's (427-347 BCE) birth, Athens was the center of the Greek world. Plato was especially influenced by Socrates, but after Athens lost the twenty-seven year Peloponnesian War, Socrates came under suspicion, eventually being condemned to death. As a result of his friend's death, Plato was forever suspicious of the rule of common people.

Socrates believed that reason could resolve philosophical questions if we employ a method of rational argument and counter-argument. Through this series of questions and answers—the Socratic Method—he showed people they didn't know what they claimed to know. Socrates claimed that he often didn't know the answers to his questions, but that he was wiser than others in knowing that he didn't know. This is Socratic wisdom. Unfortunately, questioning people and asking them to defend their beliefs often arouses hostility. We can guess that Socrates would have agreed with Spinoza who said: "I cannot teach philosophy without being a disturber of the peace." Disturbing this peace would lead to Socrates undoing.

Plato was shocked by Socrates execution, but maintained faith in rational inquiry. Plato wrote extensively, and in a series of dialogues expounded the first systematic philosophy of the Western world. While the early dialogues recount the trial and death of Socrates, most of the rest of the dialogues portray Socrates questioning those who think they know the meaning of ideas like:

24

justice (in the *Republic*), moderation (in the *Charmides*), courage
(in the *Laches*), knowledge, (in the *Theaetetus*), virtue (in the
Meno), piety (in the *Euthophro*) or love (in the *Symposium*.) *The
Republic* is the most famous of the dialogues, touching on many
great philosophical issues including the best form of government,
the best life to live, the nature of knowledge, as well as family,
education, psychology and more. It also expounds Plato's Theory
of Human Nature.

Theory of Reality

Plato wasn't a theist or polytheist. When he talked of the divine,
he was referring to a rational element (logos) that organized the
world from preexisting matter. What is most distinctive about
Plato's philosophy is his theory of forms, which are ideas or
concepts having at least four aspects:

1. *Logical* –How do universal concepts like "bed" or
   "dog" or "red" apply to individual things? Notice that
   every word in the dictionary except proper names and
   pronouns refers to a concept. But do these universal
   concepts exist independently, or are there just
   particular things? Nominalists argue that words
   simply name things, there are no universal concepts;
   words are convenient names that demarcate some
   things from others. Platonic realists argue that
   universal forms exist independently. Individual dogs
   participate in the form of "dogness" which transcends
   individual dogs.

2. *Metaphysical* – Are forms ultimately real, do they
   exist independently? Plato said that universal, eternal,
   immaterial, unchanging forms are more real than
   individuals. Individual material things are known by
   the senses, whereas forms are known by the intellect.
   The forms have a real, independent existence.

3. *Epistemological* – Knowledge is of forms; perceptions lead only to belief or opinion. We find the clearest example of knowledge based on forms in mathematics. Hence the motto of Plato's academy: 'Let no one ignorant of geometry enter here." The objects of mathematical reasoning are often not found in this world—we can never see most of them—but they provide knowledge about the world. Plato challenged us to account for mathematical knowledge without positing mathematical forms, and even today many mathematicians are mathematical Platonists.

4. *Moral* – Moral concepts like justice and equality are forms. Individuals and societies can participate in justice, liberty, or equality, but in this world we never encounter the perfect forms. The most prominent of all the forms is the form of the "good."

Plato used three images to explain his theory of the Forms. The first is the **myth of the cave.**

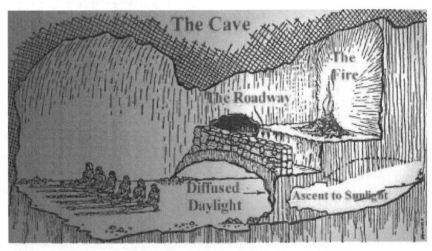

In his story, the chained prisoners see only the wall in front of them while in the roadway behind them various objects are carried back and forth resulting in shadows on the wall. One day a prisoner breaks free and sees the objects behind him. He now knows there is something more real than shadows and he has more knowledge of his reality. Eventually, he makes his way out of the cave and sees objects in the sunlight, and then he sees the sun itself.

The allegory this refers to his leaving behind the impermanent, material world for the permanent intelligible world. It is a story about the human journey from darkness to light, from sleeping to waking, from ignorance to knowledge. For Christians like St. Augustine it represented the soul's journey from this world to the heavenly one. Contemporary commentators often argue that has something to say to us. We look at our televisions, smart phones, and computer screens rather than contemplating eternal things.

Plato's next device to explain forms is the **divided line.**

Kinds of Existence	Objects The Good	Mode of Knowing
Intelligible Supernatural	Forms	noesis
	Mathematical Objects	dianoia
Sensible Natural	Things	pistis
	Images	eikasia

As we move from bottom to top we find more reality and more knowledge. For example, if we only know the shadow of a horse, we are at the bottom of Plato's line (images). The shadow has little reality—it depends on the horse casting it—and it provides little knowledge. If we now see an actual horse we have moved up one level (things). We know more about horses and the actual horse has more reality than its shadow. If we move further upward, we come to the realm of understanding (mathematical objects.) Finally, as we proceed upward we arrive at the world of forms, the highest of which is the form of the good.

Finally Plato said that just as the **sun** illuminates the entire physical world so too, by analogy, does the idea of the good illuminate all of reality. Thus the entire material, temporal world that we usually see is less real than the immaterial, non-temporal reality. I don't know if this other world exists, but if he's right dinner is not that important.

Human Nature

Plato was a *dualist*, who believed that there is both an immaterial mind (soul) and a material body. He believed that souls exist before birth and survive after death. Before we were born he thought our soul sees the forms and that learning is a matter of recalling those forms. We don't see perfect circles or perfect justice in this world, the knowledge of them comes from our preexistent state. He also believed that the soul or mind attains knowledge of the forms, as opposed to the senses, and that we should care about our soul rather than our body.

The soul (mind) itself is divided into three parts: 1) *reason; 2) appetite*; and 3) *emotion/will*. Examples of the latter include: love, anger, indignation, ambition, aggression, etc. Plato argued that when these three aspects aren't in harmony we experience mental conflict. For example, we might be pulled by passionate love, lustful appetite, or the reasoned desire to find the best partner. Plato's own image to describe the relationship of the three parts of the mind is of the charioteer who tries to control two horses pulling his chariot. The charioteer represents reason, while the horses represent emotions and appetites. Elsewhere Plato said that reason should use the will to control the appetites. Plato also emphasized the social aspect of human nature. We are not self-sufficient, and we benefit from social interactions, and from the talent and friendship of others.

The Problem

Persons differ as to which part of their nature dominates. Individual dominated by reason are philosophical and seek knowledge; individuals dominated by will or emotion are victory loving and seek reputation; individuals dominated by appetites are profit loving and seek material gain. Although each has a role to play, in harmonious minds reason rules the will and appetites. Similarly, in a harmonious or just society, the rational rule. Thus there is a parallel between proper functioning individuals and proper functioning societies. Good societies help produce good people who in turn help produce good societies, while bad societies tend to produce bad individuals who in turn help produce bad societies.

Plato differentiates five kinds of societies, each one worse than the other as we go down the following list:

1. The best is a meritocracy, where the talented rule.

2. The timarchic society values honor and fame while neglecting reason. In such a society, spirit dominates the society.

3. *Oligarchy* means that money making is valued and political power lies with the wealthy. In such a society appetites dominate.

4. *Democracy* is where the masses, dominated by their appetites, seize power. Plato described the common people as "lacking in discipline (and) pursuing mere pleasure of the moment …"

5. *Anarchy* is the sequel to the permissiveness and self-indulgence of democracy; it is the total lack of government. Plato thought this would usher in a tyrant to restore order.

The Solution

Justice is the same in both individuals and society—the harmonious workings of the parts to create a flourishing whole. But how is this attained? Plato believed that education—academic, musical, and physical—was the key. Not surprisingly he thought the rulers should be philosophers, inasmuch as in them reason dominates. If there really is a truth about how people should live, then only those with such knowledge should rule. Think of the parallels with Confucianism, where those who rule have mastered the Confucian political texts.

To achieve this end, the guardians or rulers must engage in a long educational process in which they learn about the Forms. After a nearly fifty year long process, those of the highest moral and intellectual excellence will rule. The guardians can't own personal property and can't have families. The idea is that only the desire to serve the common good motivates them, rather than money or power. Plato hoped that the guardians will so love wisdom that they wouldn't misuse their power. As for those dominated by will or emotion, they are best suited to being auxiliaries—soldiers, police, and civil servants. The final class is comprised of the majority, those in whom the appetites dominate. They will be farmers, craftsman, traders, and other producers of the materials necessary for living.

Critics have called Plato's republic authoritarian or totalitarian. He did advocate both censorship and propaganda as means of social control. He certainly believed that the masses, who he says like to shop and spend, were unable to govern the society.

Aristotle: Humans Are Material

Aristotle's Life and Work

Aristotle (384-322 BCE) was a student of Plato's and the tutor of Alexander the Great. Aristotle's background in biology made him more of an empiricist (truth discovered primarily by the senses) as compared to the mathematician Plato's rationalism (truth discovered primarily by reason.) Aristotle attended Plato's academy, but founded his own school, the Lyceum, later in his life. Both schools would exist, off and on, for between five hundred and almost a thousand years.

Aristotle wrote on an amazing range of topics including: logic, metaphysics, epistemology, astronomy, physics, meteorology, biology, psychology, ethics, politics, law, and poetics. We can safely say that Aristotle influenced more subjects for a longer period of time than any thinker in the history of humanity. His scientific ideas were often false, but they were the received wisdom for two thousand years. His logic is still used today, and his influence in multiple areas of philosophy is still felt. For our explication of Aristotle, we will mainly focus on the Nicomachean Ethics.

Theory of Reality

Aristotle is not a classical theist like Augustine or Aquinas, but he does have a conception of an unmoved mover, a cause/sustainer of the universe. This is not a personal god who cares about human beings or is the object of worship; it is more like a magnet that keeps things in motion by attracting them toward it.

Aristotle rejected Plato's belicf in independently existing forms. There is something common to things that share a concept x, but that essence/form/pattern/structure is embedded in the matter. The form is the pattern of a thing, and the matter is what makes something an individual thing. Everything in the world is a formed matter; that is matter in a certain form. You never find matter without form—which would be like primordial goo—and you never find form without matter—with the exception of the unmoved mover. Some forms are very primitive—a brick is basically just the shape of heated clay—while others are very complicated—like that of a human being.

Another way of understanding his metaphysics is to consider the four causes, or four questions we can ask about a thing: 1) *material* cause—what something is made of? 2) *formal* cause—what kind of thing is it? 3) *efficient* cause—what caused it to exist? And 4) *final* cause—what is its purpose or function? These causes do help explain human artifacts like statues or books, but the idea of a final cause is problematic, especially when applied to human beings. The reference to a final cause assumes a teleological view of reality—the idea that nature is goal-oriented—but this view has been undermined and rejected by modern science.

Human Nature

Aristotle was a materialist who organized living things into plants, animals, and human beings. Each class he thought had a different structure. Plants have a vegetative structure, a way of functioning, which is primarily about taking in nutrients and reproducing. Non-human animals have this structure plus a sensory structure, which uses the senses to interact with the environment. Humans add a rational structure on top of the vegetative and sensory structures. Thus different kinds of things have a different structure or form. In his language, this is its formal cause. And some things have a richer or more complex form than others.

So the form of something does not exist independently; it is not an entity in itself. Rather, it is the specific pattern or structure of a thing which defines how it exists and functions. It is different to be structured as a rock, tree, dog, or human. Thus, for Aristotle, it makes no sense to talk of a soul or mind without a body, for the essence of a person is embedded in their matter. You can't take it out of the body.

The only exception to this is that divine intellectual functioning may take place without a body. Yet it is hard to see how this could be the case. For example, even if computers think without bodies their thought still depends on material components. Disembodied thought is conceptually problematic, although many Christians and Islamists who followed Aristotle welcomed the possibility.

Aristotle also held that humans are social and political creatures who only reach our full development in societies. However he doesn't think that women are rational, and his remarks about them are condescending. In addition, Aristotle advanced a doctrine of natural slavery—he thought that some are naturally slaves. Nonetheless we shouldn't reject all of Aristotle's thought because he was a misogynist, racist, and imperialist. That would be an ad hominem argument.

The Problem

Rather than diagnosing a flaw in human nature and proposing a remedy, Aristotle gave us an account of the end, purpose or meaning of life and how one might achieve it. Rather than offer an otherworldly account of salvation, he offered a worldly one more akin to Confucianism or Buddhism.

Aristotle began by asking if there is one thing at which all action aims; if there is one thing all action seeks for its own sake. Aristotle said that eudemonia—variously translated as happiness, flourishing, well-being, living well, fulfillment, or perfection—was the goal of human life. In his own words "the human good turns out to be activity in the soul (mind) in accordance with excellence."

Anything, even inanimate things, can function excellently. A good pen or a good dog functions as they are supposed to. Humans have both excellences of intellect—theoretical and practical reason—and excellences of character—virtues like wisdom, temperance, courage, and justice. In general he presented these virtues as "the mean between the extremes." A life of virtue, excellence of character, is the ideal for human life. Like Plato he emphasized both moral and intellectual virtue. But unlike Socrates and Plato, who thought knowledge was sufficient for virtue, Aristotle recognized that knowing the good doesn't mean one will do the good because we might have weak wills.

The Solution

A key is that vice and virtue result from habits; which themselves result from past actions and environments, including the social and political environment. This leads us to Aristotle's conception of government and society. In brief, Aristotle believed that societies only survive and flourish if there is some basic agreement about issues of private morality. (It is hard to know his recommendation for a pluralistic society like ours. The American founders thought that individual moral and religious pluralism was allowable, as long as the public, secular good took precedence.)

As for his specific, ideal notion of the good life, Aristotle contrasted lives of pleasure, honor, and intellectual reflection. Not surprisingly, he felt that intellectual contemplation was the best human activity. Here he was on the same page as Plato, who argued that intellectual pleasures were better than physical ones. Plato said you can confirm this claim because those who have experienced both types of pleasure prefer the intellectual ones.

Aristotle on Living Well

No discussion of Aristotle's views about human nature would be complete without a brief overview of his views about the purpose of our lives. Aristotle's views on living well begin with a simple consideration of ends and means. Suppose we want a car—the car is our end, goal or purpose. We can borrow, earn, steal, or save to get the car—these are our means. The means we choose depends on which is easier, quicker, more likely to succeed, etc. Thinking about the goal we are aiming at, and the means we must employ to reach that goal is practical thinking. But such thinking bears no fruit until it results in purposeful action, which is acting with some end, goal, or purpose in mind. Purposeful action contrasts with aimless or thoughtless action, which is action with no end in view.

But suppose we get our car? Getting a car is itself a means to another end, say of getting to school or work. And getting to school or work is the means to another end, say of getting to class or the job. Such considerations led Aristotle to wonder whether there is any final or ultimate end, an end for which everything else is a means, an end that is not a means to anything else. In short, he wanted to know if there is an ultimate end, goal, or purpose for human life.

Aristotle argued that as we mature, we act less aimlessly and more purposefully. We try to develop a plan for living that unites all our various purposes. Without a plan for living, we don't know what we're trying to do or why. But Aristotle argued that—not only do we need a plan—we need the right plan; one that aims at our ultimate end. But again, what is the final end for human life, the end that all of us ought to aim for?

For Aristotle the final end of human life is to flourish, to live well, to have a good life. All acts should aim at this end. Of course in order to live at all we need food, clothing, and shelter, but living is itself the means to the end of living well. And what is living well a means to? Aristotle said that having a good life is the final end for humans; it is not a means to anything else. Things are good because they are the means to living or living well. Aristotle thought this was obvious because no one wants to live poorly.

But now another question arises: don't different people have different ideas about what a good life is? For some it may consist of accumulating wealth; for others it is having power, or being famous, or experiencing pleasure. And if people construe the good life differently, if they have different desires, how can there be a right plan for living well? How can there be one final end that all ought to seek?

To answer these questions Aristotle argued that not all desires are of the same sort. There are acquired desires, which differ between individuals, and natural desires, which are the same for all individuals. Acquired desires—say for caviar—correspond to our wants, whereas natural desires—say for food—correspond to our needs. You may want something you don't need or which is bad for you, but the things you need are always good for you. Acquired desires or wants correspond to apparent goods; things that appear good because you want them. Natural desires or needs correspond to real goods; things that are good for you whether you want them or not.

Aristotle concluded that the good life consists in the possession, over the course of a lifetime, of all those things that are really good for us. What is really good for us corresponds to the natural needs

36

that are the same for all human beings; thus what is good for one person is good for another. There is a right plan for living well. So what are the real goods that a person should seek to obtain in order to live well? According to Aristotle they are:

- bodily goods – health, vitality, vigor, and pleasure;

- external goods – food, drink, shelter, clothing, and sleep; and

- goods of the soul – knowledge, skill, love, friendship, aesthetic enjoyment, self-esteem, and honor.

The first two types of good are limited goods—we can have more of them than we need. Goods of the soul are unlimited goods—we cannot have too much of them. But surely the knowledge of the good life is insufficient to actually living a good life? So how do we go about possessing these goods?

Aristotle argued that the way to bridge the gap between knowledge of the good life and actually living it was through the development of a good moral character. And this entails developing good habits. A good habit allows us to perform certain actions without effort. We can have a good habit for hitting golf balls, playing the piano, or reading books. We can also habitually make good choices to avoid overeating or drinking too much.

Aristotle called good habits virtues or excellences. Virtues of the mind are intellectual virtues; virtues exemplified by a regular disposition to choose correctly are moral virtues. For Aristotle, moral virtue plays a special role in living well. The reason moral virtue—the habit of making the right choices—is so important is that our choices determine whether we live well. If we make too many bad choices we will not live well. So we need to develop good habits to help us obtain what is really good for us, as opposed to bad habits which lead us toward things that appear good, but may turn out to be bad. Good habits or moral virtues are the principle means to having good lives, because they allow us to habitually make the choices that both constitute and lead to good lives.

The most important moral virtues or habits are temperance, courage, and justice. Temperance or moderation keeps us from overindulging in pleasure, or seeking too much of the limited goods. Courage is the disposition to do what it takes to live a good life, and justice is the virtue that allows us to have friends and enjoy the benefits of cooperation. Yet knowledge of the good life and good habits may still not be enough to assure success because living well is not completely within our control. Why? First, because possessing some real goods, like wealth or health, is not completely within our power. Second, we didn't create the initial conditions of our birth; we can't control fate. Thus moral virtue doesn't guarantee a good life. We also need good habits, and good luck. But if we are knowledgeable, virtuous, and lucky, we can have good meaningful lives.

Aristotle on the Good Society

Aristotle didn't think we could live well alone, thus we need to consider other persons. Justice is the virtue concerned with the good of others, both of our friends and all others in society. Having friends and living in a just society greatly increases our chances of having good lives. But since all people are not friends, we need justice to bind people together. Justice intervenes when love or friendship fail, and it determines what one person has a right to expect from another. Were it not for justice, groups might not stay together, and having a good life would become more difficult.

What do others have a right to expect from us? That we keep our promises, tell the truth, return what we borrowed, pay our debts, and not steal, injure, or kill or interfere with their freedom of others. In short, others have a right to expect that we not do anything that would impede their living well, anything that would interfere with their obtaining the real goods necessary for a good life. Since they need these goods to live well, that gives them a right to expect them.

While others should expect that we not interfere with them, Aristotle didn't think that justice demanded we help others. Love or generosity may imply that we do this, but justice doesn't. Still, the state should make and enforce laws that require such action, inasmuch as the existence of the good society is important for everyone trying to live well. The end, goal, or purpose of the good state, Aristotle said, is to promote the possibility of good lives for all its citizens. When the state promotes an individual's welfare, it is indirectly promotes everyone's chance of living well.

What do we have a right to expect from others and from the state? We have a right to expect from others exactly what they have a right to expect from us—that they tell the truth, keep their promises, not kill or injure us, etc. And that's because what is good for them is also good for us. Furthermore, to live well we need association with others. This is where the obligations of the state come into play. Bad societies fail to help or actively hinder people's abilities to live well; good societies do the reverse. Just as a family is bad to the extent it lacks concern for its children's health; a society is bad for similar reasons. In both cases the institutions are not doing what we have a right to expect from them.

Thus some societies are better than others to the extent that they provide the condition in which their citizens flourish. As the point of an individual life is to live well; the point of civilization is to provide the conditions where all individuals have the opportunity to flourish. While Aristotle thought government necessary and good—since humans have a difficult time living together peacefully—some governments are better than others.

To determine whether a government is good or bad Aristotle asked three basic questions:

1. Does the government serve the common good or does it serve the selfish interests of those with power?

2. Does the government rest on the power at the ruler's disposal, or does it rest on laws that the rulers and the ruled have mutually agreed upon? and

3. If the government is constitutional, are the laws of that constitution just?

The best government is not tyrannical or despotic, and has a just constitution and just laws. Constitutional government is one of free people, whereas those ruled by a despot are subjects not citizens, and those ruled by tyrants are no better off than slaves. In short, we have a right to expect to be ruled as citizens under a government to which we have given our consent, and which allows us to have a voice in that government.

Furthermore, we have a right to expect that the state do everything in its power to promote human flourishing, to provide the conditions under which all individuals have the opportunity to live well. While achieving moral virtue or knowledge may be largely within our power, other goods like wealth or health may be largely determined by fortune. While a good government can't guarantee that citizens will attain moral virtue or have good lives, it can provide the condition under which this is possible, and it can help alleviate much of the injustice caused by misfortune.

Epictetus: Humans Can Control Their Thoughts

Epictetus' Life and Works

Epictetus (c. 55 – 135 CE) was born as a slave in the Roman Empire, but obtained his freedom as a teenager. He studied Stoic philosophy from an early age, eventually lecturing on Stoicism in Rome. He was forced to leave the city in 89 CE, after the Emperor Domitian banished philosophers from Italy. He then established his own school at Nicopolis on the Adriatic coast in Greece, where he taught and lectured until he died around 135. While he never married, he did adopt a child whose parents could not provide for its maintenance. Today he is regarded as one of the preeminent Stoic philosophers.

The major compilation of Epictetus' teaching is the four-volume work usually called the *Discourses*. They were not written by Epictetus, but transcribed and compiled by his pupil Arrian. Nonetheless, we have good reasons to believe that they are representative of Epictetus' thinking. His other major work is the shorter *Enchiridion* (usually referred to as the *Manual* or *Handbook*). It is essentially an abridged edition of the *Discourses*. However, the *Discourses* provide a better guide to understanding the thought of Epictetus.

Theory of Reality & Human Nature

Epictetus believed that humans were rational beings living in a rational universe. He refers to the fundamental orderliness of all things, or the rational principle underlying the universe as Zeus, god, or the gods. This rational principle pervades all reality, and we can understand rationality in Zeus conceived of as a person. As rational beings our minds are fragments of Zeus' mind, thus we are parts of Zeus. While this may sound strange to our ears, a modern interpretation says that Epictetus held that nature is intelligible, mathematical, logical or fundamentally rational.

The capacity to choose is the fundamental characteristic of human beings—the essence of our human nature. It is our volition that makes us responsible for our own actions and mental states. Thus our decisions are, by definition, free of external compulsion. This means that our convictions, attitudes, intentions and actions are ours in a way that nothing else is.

The Problem of Life & Its Solution

The basic problem in human life is that we suffer because we fail to distinguish between what is in our control and what is not. Some things are within our control: our judgments, intentions, desires, and aversions. This is the internal realm of the mind which is governed by our own volition. Everything else about us—our body, possessions, relationships, wealth, fame, reputation—is contingent on factors largely beyond our control. This is the external world governed by cause and effect. The root of our suffering is confusing the internal, over which we have control, and the external, over which we don't.

To make matters worse, we often assume that external objects and circumstances are the most valuable things in life. And when the external world doesn't meet our expectations, we experience grief, fear, envy, desire, and anxiety, all resulting from the mistaken belief that happiness is to be found outside of us. But Epictetus rejects the view that such emotions are imposed on us by external or internal forces. We are responsible for our feelings, thoughts and actions. The circumstances of our lives are but the arena in which we exercise our volition.

This basic idea of Epictetus and Stoicism in general is sometimes captured in the pithy phrase: "Happiness is not getting what we want, but wanting what we get." The idea is that well-being doesn't derive from the possession of external things, but by controlling internal states of mind. To better understand this, consider a simple example. Suppose we are stuck in traffic. We can fume and curse as our blood pressure rises or we can be thankful for the opportunity to listen to our favorite music. We have no control over the traffic, but we do have control over how we respond to it.

For Epictetus the key to inner well-being is to align what life give us with what we want or, in his language, align our will with the will of the gods:

> But I have never been hindered in my will, nor compelled when I did not will. And how is this possible? I have placed my movements toward action in obedience to God. Is it His will that I shall have fever? It is my will also. Is it His will that I should move toward anything? It is my will also. Is it His will that I should obtain anything? It is my wish also. Does He not will? I do not wish. Is it His will that I be put to the rack? It is my will then to die; it is my will then to be put to the rack. Who, then, is still able to hinder me contrary to my own judgment, or to compel me? No more than he can hinder or compel Zeus. (*The Discourses*, Book IV, Chapter 1)

These are strong claims indeed, but it seems that even under torture Epictetus was able to control his response by aligning his wants with his fate. In modern times, U.S. Navy airman James Stockdale credited the philosophy of Epictetus with helping him endure more than seven years as a prisoner of war in Vietnam. Thankfully most of us will never have to endure torture, but many of us are tormented by fear and anxiety. Here again Epictetus has something to offer. The psychologist Albert Ellis, the founder of Rational Emotive Behavior Therapy, a form of today's popular cognitive behavioral therapy, credited Epictetus with providing a foundation for his system of psychotherapy. Perhaps then there is still much to learn from this ancient philosophy.

Epictetus even extended this analysis to feelings of anger or betrayal toward others. What others do is external to us; we only have control over our response. What others do doesn't hurt us—unless we let it. Suppose someone tells us we are worthless, incompetent, or unlovable. Does this hurt us? Not unless we let it. The words are just sounds in the world. Why should they hurt us? The wind and the ocean make sounds that don't hurt us. We could let sound of the wind hurt us. We could say "I'm no good because I'm in the wind's way!" But the wind's blowing doesn't make you in the way anymore than someone telling you are stupid makes you stupid. These things only hurt you if you let them. This is what Epictetus is teaching, and it is one of the most valuable lessons in the history of thought.

Still, learning to control our minds in this way takes effort and training. A teacher can help train our minds, but we can do it ourselves too because we are rational. We can realize the difference between our minds, over which we have control, and the external world over which we do not. With effort we can even learn to alter our emotional dispositions. Still, as Spinoza warned, "all noble things are as difficult as they are rare." The journey to enlightenment and inner peace is as difficult to follow as the razor's edge.

Concluding Remarks

There is much more we could say about Epictetus and the other Stoic philosophers like Seneca and Marcus Aurelius, and I encourage everyone to read them. But perhaps the essence of Stoicism was most succinctly captured by Rene Descartes in the third maxim which governed his life. And when Descartes refers below to "such philosophers as in former times," he refers to Stoic philosophers like Epictetus.

> My third maxim was to endeavor always to conquer myself rather than fortune, and change my desires rather than the order of the world, and in general, accustom myself to the persuasion that, except our own thoughts, there is nothing absolutely in our power; so that when we have done our best in things external to us, all wherein we fail of success is to be held, as regards us, absolutely impossible: and this single principle seemed to me sufficient to prevent me from desiring for the future anything which I could not obtain, and thus render me contented; for since our will naturally seeks those objects alone which the understanding represents as in some way possible of attainment, it is plain, that if we consider all external goods as equally beyond our power, we shall no more regret the absence of such goods as seem due to our birth, when deprived of them without any fault of ours, than our not possessing the kingdoms of China or Mexico, and thus making, so to speak, a virtue of necessity, we shall no more desire health in disease, or freedom in imprisonment, than we now do bodies incorruptible as diamonds, or the wings of birds to fly with.

> But I confess there is need of prolonged discipline and frequently repeated meditation to accustom the mind to view all objects in this light; and I believe that in this chiefly consisted the secret of the power of such philosophers as in former times were enabled to rise superior to the influence of fortune, and, amid suffering and poverty, enjoy a happiness which their gods might have envied.

For, occupied incessantly with the consideration of the limits prescribed to their power by nature, they became so entirely convinced that nothing was at their disposal except their own thoughts, that this conviction was of itself sufficient to prevent their entertaining any desire of other objects; and over their thoughts they acquired a sway so absolute, that they had some ground on this account for esteeming themselves more rich and more powerful, more free and more happy, than other men who, whatever be the favors heaped on them by nature and fortune, if destitute of this philosophy, can never command the realization of all their desires.

Kant: Humans Are Rational and Free

The Cultural Milieu

Christianity dominated the social, political, and religious life of Europe for more than a thousand years, from the fall of Rome until at least the 17th century. The first major division of Christianity occurred with the schism of 1054, when the Eastern Orthodox Church broke from the western Catholic Church. But four successive cultural movements slowly unraveled the hegemony of the Catholic Church: the Renaissance, the Reformation, the 17th century scientific revolution, and the Enlightenment.

The *Renaissance* refers to the flowering of reason and humanism, literally "the rebirth" or rediscovery of Greek and Roman thought. The next great cultural movement was the *Reformation*, begun when Martin Luther (1483 – 1546) posted his ninety-five thesis on the door of his German church. There had been other reforming voices before Luther, such as John Wycliffe and John Hess, but Luther's protest really started the Reformation. (Both Wycliffe, who was one of the first to translate the Bible into English, and

Huss met terrible fates. Huss was burned at the stake, while Wycliffe was declared a heretic, his works burned and his remains exhumed and burned. William Tyndale, another of the early translators of the Bible was also burned at the stake.)

Luther had many disagreements with the Church, especially its selling of indulgences which told people to believe they could buy their way into heaven. By contrast Luther believed that we are saved by faith and grace, without the need for the Church as an intermediary between god and humans. He also rejected reason which he famously called a whore. Thus he rejected both the Church, its scholasticism (using reason in theology) and the rise of reason associated with the Renaissance. He emphasized the scripture as a truer source of religious truth than the Church.

This religious reform—especially the emphasis on faith and the authority of the Bible—spread throughout northern Europe. The emphasis on scripture was particularly strong in the thought of John Calvin, who helped develop a theocratic state in Geneva. These ideas spread with the puritans to England and then to America, where the doctrine of the infallibility of the Bible was developed. (St. Augustine didn't even believe this!) Of course the issue of Biblical interpretation soon arose. In response, some sects like the Quakers emphasized religious experience. All of this led to centuries of violent conflict and genocide between various religious groups. Of course today Europe is almost completely secular, while America is overtly religious.

The next great cultural movement was *the 17th century scientific revolution*. This revolution truly changed the world, just look around you to see its overwhelming influence. The combination of Francis Bacon's (1561 – 1626) experimental method, and the mathematical reasoning used by Galileo (1564 – 1642) and Newton (1642 – 1727) showed that science could explain the heavens and the earth. This implied that appealing to the Bible and the Church in matters of science was futile, as the trial of Galileo would eventually show. But how far can a scientific approach go in explaining human beings? Are we material only, or is there some immaterial component to us? These questions were of great interest during the *Enlightenment*, which lasted from the mid-seventeenth to the late eighteenth century. Enlightenment thinkers emphasized reason, analysis, and individuality rather than traditional authorities like the Church. This is the cultural milieu into which Kant is born.

Kant's Life and Work

Immanuel Kant (1724 - 1804) is generally considered one of the three or four greatest philosophers in the Western tradition. He lived his entire life in Konigsberg, Prussia which is today the city of Kaliningrad in Russia. Kant's philosophy is extraordinarily complex, but he was particularly interested in reconciling Christianity with the science of the Enlightenment.

Kant himself was an accomplished scientist who developed the first account of the origin of the solar system. His education in the humanities was equally impressive. He knew Greek and Latin philosophy and literature, as well as European philosophy, theology, and political theory. In his university education he was particularly influenced by Leibniz, a rationalist who believed that reason could prove both the existence of god and that we live in the best of all possible worlds. Kant's philosophy attempted to reconcile such rationalism with the empiricism of figures like Hobbes and Hume.

Kant was the deepest thinker of the European Enlightenment, and he used reason to examine everything, even the traditional and the sacred. His motto was that of the Enlightenment, "dare to think." He argued that the only limits on human reason are those that we

48

discover when we scrutinize reason. His emphasis on the inquiry into the nature and limits of human knowledge meant that epistemology became for him the heart of philosophy. And he turned his critical analysis to science, metaphysics, ethics, judgments of beauty, and to religion.

Theory of Reality

Kant tried to explain how scientific knowledge was possible. In the first part of his *Critique of Pure Reason*, Kant set out his theory of space, time, substance, causality and more. He also argued that science depends on certain fundamental presuppositions—every event has a cause, something is conserved during the process of change, etc. These presuppositions make the experience of an objective, external world possible and hence, Kant reasoned, the presuppositions of science are probably true. Finally, after a long argument he concluded that mathematical and scientific knowledge are justified.

Kant also accepted the existence of an independently existing material world, yet he argued that perception of the external world depends on how the inputs from that world are processed by our cognitive faculties and sensory apparatus. This implies that our cognitive intuitions may "distort our representation of what exists." Thus we know the world only as it appears to us, not as it really is. This is Kant's Copernican revolution. We are at the center of our reality, structuring it with our minds; our minds are not passive receptors of the external world. And in the process of structuring reality, we may come to have a distorted view of reality.

In the second part of the *Critique of Pure Reason*, Kant argued that reason goes beyond its proper role when it claims knowledge of metaphysical things like souls and God. So Kant rejected natural theology; for him theology was not an intellectually justified discipline. Many theologians have responded with fideism but

Kant was not in this tradition. He would need other ways to justify ethics and religion. Thus Kant is skeptical of *any* theory of reality; we can't know reality.

Human Nature

So what of Kant's conception of human nature? Are we body and soul or merely material? Kant thought that reason can't resolve this question. What about freedom? Regarding our bodies, we are just as determined as anything in the physical world, but because we are rational beings, we are free to act using reason. Kant doesn't solve the problem of freedom—nobody else has either—but he believed that we act "under the idea of freedom." In other words, it is practical to believe that we are free, and the ethical point of view presupposes freedom as well. We are free, rational creatures. But if we are free, rational creatures, what should we choose to do?

The Problem

Kant contrasted non-human animals, which have desires but no sense of duty, with humans who experience tension between their self-interested desires and the demands of duty. We should do our duty, yet we have a propensity to be immoral. As for the source of immorality, Kant believed that we freely choose to disregard our duty and, at the same time, the tendency to do evil is partly innate. The extent to which society exacerbates our evil proclivities is debatable, but we can say that something is amiss in human life. We have a duty to others, but we are self-interested. The problem of life is how to be moral given our tendency to be immoral.

The Solution

Kant said that the only thing that is completely good is a good will—the desire of the will to conform itself to the moral law. But how do we overcome selfishness and act morally? Kant dismissed self-interested reasons to be moral—you will be punished if you don't act appropriately—because such reasons are inconsistent with virtue. Instead, Kant argued that reason demands that we be moral, even when moral demands conflict with self-interest. We should follow the moral law, and disregard whatever consequences may follow. But if we subordinate our moral duty to our inclinations, to the desire for our own happiness, then we violate the moral law.

Kant also argued that the highest good is a combination of moral virtue and happiness. Yet morality is not always rewarded in this life, and evildoers often flourish. It is important that we have hope that moral virtue will be rewarded, although we are moral not because of possible rewards, but because being moral is our duty. While Kant didn't take a lot of religious imagery literally, he did hope that justice somehow prevailed. Yet Kant didn't emphasize a god as a solution to the moral problem rather he emphasized how practical reason justifies morality. How did he do that?

The Solution Expanded

Kant said that pure reason can't decide things like whether gods, freedom, or immortal souls are real. And if reason can't say much about metaphysics, what can it say about ethics? The key to ethics is to consider practically reasoning, reasoning about how to act.

While Kant's ethics is notoriously complex, his most basic presupposition regarding ethics is a belief in human freedom. As we said previously, while the natural world operates according to laws of cause and effect, the moral world operates according to self-imposed "laws of freedom." Here is his basic argument for freedom:

1. Without freedom, morality is not possible.

2. Morality exists, thus

3. Freedom exists.

The first premise is true because determinism undermines morality. The second premise Kant takes as self-evident, and the conclusion follows from the premises. Kant also believes that freedom comes from rationality. Here is his argument:

1. Without reason, we would be slaves to our passions
2. If we were slaves to our passions, we would not be free; thus
3. Without reason, we would not be free.

We now have the basis upon which to connect between reason and morality.

1. Without reason, there is no freedom
2. Without freedom, there is no morality, thus
3. Without reason, there is no morality.

Thus Kant believed moral obligation derived from our free, rational nature. But how should we exercise our freedom? What should we choose to do? Since we are free, rational beings we can choose between actions. Moral actions are actions where reason leads rather than follows, actions freely chosen by our desire to follow the moral law. Again, the moral law ultimately comes from God, but it can be known by any rational person.

So how do we know the moral law? Kant assumed that there must be some rational representation of the moral law. And when he thought about laws, one of their key characteristics is that they are universal. So the moral law must be characterized by its universality. Just as an equation of the form $a (b + c) = ab + ac$ is universally applicable, the moral law must have an abstract formulation too. His most famous formulation of the moral law is that we should act according to a principle which we can universalize with consistency. This is what he calls the *categorical imperative*. (Essentially we ask of any action, "what if everybody did this?")

By asking this question about proposed actions, we can determine if they are moral. If we can universalize our actions with consistency, then they are moral; if we cannot, they are immoral. For example, there is no logical inconsistency in universalizing the principle, whenever we need money we will work hard to earn the money. So Kant believed this action was moral. But there is something inconsistent about universalizing the maxim, whenever we need money we should rob a bank. Such acts are immoral because the bank robber is willing a world where:

a. banks exist as the necessary prerequisite of the bank robbery intended, and

b. banks don't exist as the necessary consequence of bank robberies.

So Kant's basic idea is something like this. If I say you can taste my wine, then I should be able to taste yours. This is a simple demand of rational consistency. Of course, we can act contrary to reason because we are free. The bank robber probably won't stop robbing banks when we tell him about Kantian moral philosophy, and anyone can say that $2 + 2 = 6$, or that round squares exist. But we violate reason when we do or say these things.

In summary, we act ethically if we conform our free will to the moral law. We understand the moral law as the categorical imperative—an imperative that doesn't depend on our desires, but which prescribes action that is rationally consistent. If we follow the dictates of reason we will act morally. This may not lead to happiness, but we will have done our duty. We will have acted as free, moral, rational beings.

Finally, if Kant ethics seems too formalistic, let me add a final thought. Kant also believed in the continual progress in human culture through education, economic development, and political reform. He believed that together these forces could emancipate people from poverty, war, ignorance, and subjection to traditional authorities. He supported egalitarian and democratic ideals, imagining a world of peaceful cooperation between peoples. And Kant expressed hope that human potential could be gradually fulfilled. He believed in our reason and our freedom; a rational, free nature was the highest expression of our nature. He was a consummate Enlightenment thinker.

Sartre: Humans Are Radically Free

The Existential Tradition

Jean-Paul Sartre (1905 -1980) was both France's most important philosopher for much of the twentieth-century, as well as an important novelist and playwright. He is classified as an existentialist, which implies that his philosophy takes particular interest in: 1) the uniqueness of an individual life, not abstract theories about a shared human nature; 2) the meaning of life from a subjective point of view; and 3) the freedom to choose one's projects, meanings, and values. To better grasp existentialism, here is a brief sketch of a few of the philosophers who influenced Sartre.

The Danish philosopher, Christian Soren Kierkegaard (1813 – 1855) is usually thought of as the first existentialist, though there is an existential dimension in many previous Christian thinkers, especially Augustine and Pascal. Like Marx, Kierkegaard rejected Hegel's abstruse metaphysics, focusing instead on individuals and their choices. Kierkegaard believed that people typically: a) search for pleasure; b) commit to family, work, and social responsibility;

or c) concentrate on the divine. He thought the latter life was the best.

The other seminal figure in existentialism is the atheist Friedrich Nietzsche (1844 -1900), famous for declaring that "god is dead." He believed that religion no longer plays a significant role in western culture. We have seen through its illusions, and need to find the meaning of life without invoking gods. He also thought that we must create our own values. We must become supermen who reject conventional, religious values and exert our will to power.

Sartre's Life and Work

Much of Sartre's work originated from and was influenced by his experiences as a Frenchman in Nazi occupied France. His focus on choice was surely influenced by the choice that all French faced between collaboration, resistance, or quiet self-preservation. He later became a Marxist, joining the Communist Party in the early 1950s, although left it over the Soviet invasion of Hungary in 1956. Sartre was politically active until late in life, supporting exploited workers, nascent political revolutions and condemning American aggression in Vietnam. His thinking can be divided into two phases, the first, which focused on individual freedom, and the second, which investigated the social and economic limitations on human freedom. It seems his early bedrock belief in freedom was shaken by the reality of the social and economic world.

Metaphysics

Sartre distinguished human consciousness and inanimate non-consciousness, between "two modes of being." One is the way conscious beings exist—what he calls being for itself—the other how non-conscious things exist—what he calls being in itself. While this distinction raises many technical issues in Sartre's philosophy, for our purposes the key is that human consciousness is unique. The other main foundation of Sartre's thought is his atheism. The main implication for Sartre is that there are no transcendent values, and no intrinsic meaning or purpose for our lives. Life is absurd, we are forlorn. We have to grow up and choose our own values and projects—the meaning of life isn't something discovered, but something we create.

Human Nature

Sartre didn't believe in a human nature that precedes us. Rather, we exist as concrete individuals and then choose to create our nature. Nothing, not god or evolution, created us for any purpose; the only purpose we have is the one we give ourselves. Of course Sartre recognized that we are biological beings, but there are no general truths about what we should or ought to be. The most basic thing we can say about humans is that they are radically free; they are free to be anything, except to not be free. They can choose anything except they can't choose not to choose. In his words, we are "condemned to be free."

Thus Sartre rejected Freud's psychic determinism as well as the idea of the unconscious. Sartre believed we choose our mental states, even though some emotions for example seem to be part of our nature. He also thought that character traits are choices. We are not shy, we choose to be shy. This too seems only partly true. Still he believed that our freedom was evident when we make resolutions. We may say we'll start a diet on Monday, but when Monday rolls around and we're confronted with cookies—we face human freedom. Past resolution have no power.

The Problem

When we confront our freedom, we experience anxiety. We may try to avoid the angst that accompanies freedom by denying our freedom. But we can't escape freedom, we must choose because we are condemned to be free. Think about the anxiety of choice. What job should we do? Who should we marry? Where should we live? What should we believe? To believe that we can escape choice is to act in bad faith in Sartre's language. It is a kind of self-deception to imagine that our thoughts and actions are determined. You could be an axe murderer or join the Peace Corps; you could be an atheist or believer. In Sartre's examples a woman acts in bad faith when she doesn't recognize her freedom to resist a man's seductions; and a waiter acts in bad faith if he assumes that he must act like a waiter. The woman is not an object to be seduced, and the man is not essentially a waiter. Our own decisions govern what we do or think, and we are responsible for them.

Sartre rejected the view that Freudian repression explained bad faith. For if there is a censor in the mind that represses, it must decide what to repress and what not to, so it must be aware of what's repressed. But this is contradictory. Bad faith is a description of a whole person, not some part of their mind. Still, to say we act in good faith is also problematic because we are not essentially anything. If we act gay, shy or arrogant, we are choosing to do so. We are not essentially shy, gay, or arrogant. To make such claims is to act in bad faith. What we should say is that we choose to be gay, shy or arrogant.

As for others, Sartre thought we can infer that they have minds. When other people look at us, we know we are being observed, hence we experience emotions like shame or pride. Other people look at us and objectify us, and thus threaten our freedom. Thus humans engage in power struggles since we have a hard time accepting the freedom of others. This was Sartre at his bleakest. Clearly though there is a tension between Sartre's claim on the one hand that we are radically free, and on the other hand that in relationships with others we try to deny or possess their freedom.

Why can't we choose not to be objects or to make objects of others?

The Solution

Sartre rejected objective values so there is no specific way of life he can recommend. What he can do is condemn bad faith and praise making "our individual choices with fully self-conscious, "anguished" awareness that nothing determines them." This means accepting responsibility for everything else about ourselves, while rejecting the idea that there are objective values to which we must adhere.

Sartre showed how objective values and ethical theories don't help in situations where we must choose. He asks: should a man go off to fight the Nazis or stay home and care for his mother? No moral theory, intuition, or emotion tells you what to do. You must simply exercise your freedom and choose. To say that some moral principle forces you to do one thing or another is to act in bad faith, it denies your freedom. He was right that moral theories don't answer all moral questions, but that is different than saying we should do whatever we want.

Sartre said we should act authentically, recognizing that we are free to act in different ways, and responsible for our actions. Today such assertions fly in the face of research about how genes and environment influence our mental processes and behaviors. But he maintained that self-knowledge entails understanding the reasons, not the causes, of our actions and beliefs. But is authentic choice all there is to it? If so, it would seem Sartre would have to commend a dedicated Nazi, Dick Cheney and other members of the George W. Bush administration involved with torture. And he would also have to condemn people who do good things because they believe in objective values. So an ethics which boils down to "just choose" seems incomplete at best.

Freedom for Everyone

As Sartre's thought developed, he came to believe that freedom was situated within the contexts of facts about human beings— their *facticity*. Our freedom is limited by our bodies—I will never play in the NFL or NBA—and our place in history and society—I will not inherit 20 billion dollars like the Walton heirs. So some human beings are freer than others. Some have the chance to go to Harvard and become physicians, but most do not. So Sartre pulled back on the idea of freedom as his thought matured.

Sartre also came to believe that human relationships could be authentic. If others see us as free, they give meaning to our life just as we give it to our own lives. He even argued there can be authentic love. Perhaps he was experiencing the wisdom and maturity that comes with age. Regardless, he concluded that to be authentic was to recognize the freedom of all people, which best obtains in a socialist, classless society where all are able to express their freedom. Thus he encouraged us to use our freedom to change both ourselves and the world. This is Sartre at his most inspiring.

Chapter 3 – Scientific Theories of Human Nature

Marx: Human Life Is Determined By Economics

Marx's Life and Work

We begin with a disclaimer. We are interested in Marxist theory, not in the various ways it may have been implemented. (Think of the parallel with Christianity. If someone says Christians conducted the Crusades and the Inquisition, collaborated with the Nazis and pedophile priests, and condemn disbelief for all eternity, you might answer that none of that is Christian behavior. A Marxist can say the same about Stalin or Mao.) Who was Karl Marx (1818 – 1883)? Marx was the greatest critical theorist of the Industrial Revolution and nineteenth-century capitalism. He was hostile to religion, yet he believed in human equality and freedom, and he believed that scientific method could solve the problems of human society. He was a prophet of secular salvation.

Marx studied at the University of Berlin in the mid nineteenth-century at a time and place when G.W.F. Hegel's thought was dominant. Hegel believed in a progressive human history where *Geist* (mind, spirit or god) develops throughout history. All of human history is "the progressive self-realization of *Geist*." The idea is that human social life evolves in a progressive direction leading to greater consciousness, self-awareness and freedom. Hegel believed that mental and cultural development eventually reaches a state of absolute knowledge. Right Hegelians believed that the 19th Prussian state had reached a near perfect state of development; left Hegelians believed it had not, that the society was far from ideal and it was up to people to make it better.

For the relevance of all this consider politics in the USA today. Conservatives from the right argue that "the USA is the greatest nation ever," "America, love it or leave it," "God loves America most," etc. Thus change is unnecessary. From the left comes the idea that there is much unfilled promise, thus the need for a progressive political program. Conservatives want to conserve—discrimination against homosexuals—or go backward—get rid of social security, women in the labor force, minimum wage, contraception, labor unions, inheritance taxes, Medicare, Medicaid, etc. Liberals want to liberate—free people from undue burdens, lack of health care, minimum wage jobs, unwanted pregnancies, etc.

The other main influence on Marx was Ludwig Feuerbach. Rather than thinking that Geist realizes itself throughout history, humans created religion as an idealized version of the poor conditions in this world. In other words, this world is so bad that people imagine another perfect world. Feuerbach also used another idea of Hegel's. Hegel had developed the idea of alienation in which subjects confront objects unknown and alien from themselves. Feuerbach argued that people become alienated when "they project their own human potential into theological fantasies and undervalue their actual lives." Feuerbach argued that metaphysics and theology are expressions of our emotions disguised as claims about reality. In short, religion is a symptom of human alienation. So in order to be happy we must free ourselves from religion, and fulfill our destiny to make this world better.

All this led Marx to conclude that Hegel was right to be concerned about progress in history, but he was wrong to think the natural, historical world was a manifestation of the development of spirit or mind. Instead, Marx argued, mind is a manifestation of the natural world—hence the idea that Marx turned Hegel upside down. The driving force of social change is not ideas about gods or cosmic spirits, as Hegel thought, but economic conditions. Alienation is not religious; it is social and economic. In a capitalist system we are alienated from our labor because we work for others who own both the means of production and the products of our labor as private property. Capitalists maximize profit, exploiting their workers by paying them the minimum needed for their survival.

Theory of Reality

Marx was an atheist, a materialist, and a social scientist who thought he had discovered a scientific way to study economic history. He was looking for general socio-economic laws that applied to human history, both synchronically and diachronically.

At any given time, synchronically, economics determines ideology. The rich and powerful defend capitalism because it serves their interests. Their rhetoric regarding freedom of enterprise, trade, and markets expresses the interests of those who have property and capital. The rest are left "free to starve," if the labor markets won't give them jobs. Marx thought that social, legal, and political power was in the hands of capitalists, especially the very wealthy. He would not be surprised that in a rich country like America today, the capitalists and financiers try to prevent government attempts to reign in their excess profits, or their contributions to climate change and environmental degradation.

Looking across time, diachronically, Marx recognized that economic and technological development will result in social, political and ideological change. Consider how agriculture, slavery, feudalism, or the industrial revolution transformed social and political life. Marx's salient insight is that a materialist theory of history explains these changes.

> In the social production of their existence, men inevitably enter into definite relations, which are independent of their will ... The totality of these relations of production constitutes the economic structure of society, the real foundation, on which arises a legal and political superstructure and to which correspond definite forms of social consciousness. The mode of production of material life conditions the general process of social, political and intellectual life. It is not the consciousness of men that determines their existence, but their social existence that determines their consciousness ...

The economic base of a society provides the foundation of one's social life, and it determines that social life to a great extent. To better understand all this consider the distinctions Marx drew between:

a. *Material powers of production*: natural resources— land, climate, plants, animals, minerals; technology—tools, machinery, communication systems; human resources—labor power and skills.

b. *Economic Structure*: the organizational structure of work, division of labor, authority in the workplace, legal power of ownership, systems of rewards and payments, legal concepts of property, economic concepts like money, capital, and wages.

c. *Ideological Superstructure*: social beliefs, morality, laws, politics, religion, and philosophy.

It is not exactly clear what Marx meant by economics being the basis of social life, but clearly economics influences ideology— surely we have to eat before we can think! So Marx is right, the economic structure determines how you *can* earn your bread in a society, and thus the way most people act or think a large part of the time. For instance, if you earn money selling cigarettes, crude oil, real estate, alcohol, or assault weapons, that influences how you think about those things. Or if you grow up in a sub-culture with few economic opportunities, you will think differently about occupations like small time drug dealer, prostitute, and professional boxing, law enforcement, courts, laws, or foreign wars. Consider the vastly different political views of different socio-economic classes.

Marx thought that capitalism would become gradually more unstable, class struggle would increase, and economic inequality would skyrocket. (These themes were part of the subject of Thomas Piketty's recent worldwide best-seller. Piketty argues that capital in the hands of the wealthy will always increase faster than labor share's of that capital. In response, he proposes a global wealth tax. Consider how your own reaction to this is largely determined by your own socio-economic background.) The extent to which Marx's predictions have come true is open to debate. On the one hand, capitalism more or less reigns in first world countries; on the other hand the strengthening of the social safety net in these countries may have prevented the kind of upheaval that Marx envisioned.

Human Nature

Marx was more interested in the social nature of humans than their biological nature, since our actions presuppose the existence of other people, and what we do is affected by interacting with others in society. What seems 'instinctive' in one society or epoch—for example, a certain role for women—may be different in another. Thus for Marx sociology is not reducible to biology or psychology. Some things about humans *cannot* be explained by facts about individuals, but must be explained by society.

Who Are We?

The Problem

Estrangement in Marx refers to our alienation from other people, as well as from the products and process of our labor. Without capital, we must sell our labor to capitalists who dictate the nature of work. We don't generally get to express or elaborate ourselves through our work; instead we work to satisfy our basic needs. At work we don't belong to ourselves; rather, we are under the control of others. And competing with others in a capitalist system brings us into conflict with those with whom we should feel solidarity. Alienation leads to a lack of community, to a place where individuals can't see their work as contributing to the larger society. In short, Marx saw the economic structure of capitalism as unjust.

Surprisingly many of Marx insights coincide with those of Adam Smith, the father of capitalism. Smith too was alarmed by the injustice of capitalism: "No society can surely be flourishing and happy of which by far the greater part of the numbers are poor and miserable." In Marx's time, wealthy industrialists used people for profit, including both children and adults who worked long hours in unsafe conditions. The conditions were never ameliorated by capitalists, but by responsive governments. Even today exploitation of workers, in the most advanced countries, still takes place. (The countries that treat their workers best are the social democracies of Scandinavia and Western Europe.) Furthermore, Marx believed that his analysis applies, not only to factory or minimum wage workers, but to the vast majority of people who can't fulfill their human potential, who can't express or elaborate themselves through their labor. Human beings shouldn't exist as cogs in a productive machine; they are not automata.

The Solution

If alienation and exploitation are the social problems caused by the capitalism, then the solution is to abolish that system and replace it. A more modest proposal would preserve it, but improve its obvious flaws—encouraging mindless consumption, exploitation of individuals, destruction of the environment, etc. But Marx thought a more radical change was necessary, and that the movement of history would eventually undermine capitalism. He believed that we should act to bring about the transition from capitalism to communism, a classless society in which all wealth and property are jointly owned. Marx held that a complete revolution was necessary to undermine capitalism, and create a more just and equitable society. (In fact many of the Marx's proposals have been adopted by capitalist countries—pure laissez-faire capitalism exists nowhere on the planet.)

Marx envisaged a regeneration of humanity and human societies. If human consciousness could be altered, then freedom could become real, with individuals free to actualize their potentials. The guiding principle of this world is "from each according to (their) ability, to each according to (their) needs." If this sounds idealistic, think of the voluntary labor that produced Wikipedia, YouTube, and Facebook. Marx advocated improving life, shortening work, universal education, society in balance with nature, and more. Marxism offers a hopeful vision of a human future.

Still we might object that economic factors are only one of many obstacles in the way of human fulfillment. Existential angst, immorality, illness, aggression, incarceration, mortality and more also stand in its way.

Freud: Humans Are Irrational

Freud's Life and Work

Freud's psychoanalytic approach to the mind revolutionized our understanding of human nature. Freud (1856 – 1939) grew up in Vienna where he lived until the last year of his life. He was an outstanding student with a broad range of academic interests; he attended the University of Vienna medical school, and worked as a physician before setting up a private practice in nervous disorders at the age of thirty. He continued that work for the rest of his life.

In the first phase of his career, Freud advanced some original hypotheses about the nature of neurosis, and began to develop his method for treating psychic ailments. From his early experiences conducted with middle-class Viennese woman, he hypothesized that emotional symptoms had their roots in long-forgotten emotional trauma. This trauma needed to be recalled so that the emotions associated with it could be discharged. This was the beginning of the idea of psychoanalysis. Freud often found that patients reported their trauma originated in sexual abuse—although he was uncertain how often these reports were reliable. He also postulated that psychology had a physical basis in the brain, although neurophysiology wasn't developed enough at the time to confirm this.

Around the turn of the century, he also began to formulate his theories about the sexuality of infants and the interpretation of dreams. Ideas common to our lexicon would subsequently arise— resistance, repression, and transference. Such ideas were applied to everyone's mental life, and thus a new psychological theory originated. Starting around 1920, Freud made changes to his theories introducing the death and life instincts, as well as his division of the mind into the id, ego, and superego. In later years he wrote his most philosophical works: *The Future of an Illusion*

67

argued that religion was both false and infantile, while *Civilization and Its Discontents* claimed that there was conflict between individual drives and societal morals. Freud escaped Austria before the start of World War II, and died a year later in London. Freud suffered terribly from cancer of the jaw in the final months of his life. On September 21 and 22 his doctor administered the doses of morphine, as Freud requested, resulting in Freud's death on September 23rd 1939.

Theory of Reality

Freud began his career as a physiologist who explained phenomena scientifically. He had no use for theology or metaphysics, believing instead that the human condition could be improved by the application of science and reason. Living post-Darwin, Freud recognized that human beings were animals related to all living things. He was also a materialist regarding mind—as almost all philosophers and scientists are today. In other words, he believed that mental states, including unconscious states, are dependent upon brain states. He left the project of discovering the relationship of mental states and the brain to future scientists, a project that has developed enormously since then.

Human Nature

The *first* major idea that influenced Freud's theory of human nature was determinism. This would seem to imply that humans don't possess free will, but Freud was ambivalent about that. On the one hand, he thought the contents of consciousness are determined by individual, psychological and biological drives, while on the other hand, he seemed to think we sometimes make rational decisions and judgments. This is similar to Marx's view, although Marx held that the causes of the contents of our consciousness were primarily social and economic.

The *second* key idea in Freud's theorizing was the postulation of the unconscious. For Freud there are not only preconscious states—those we can recall even if we aren't continually conscious—but unconscious states that can't ordinarily become conscious of. Our minds contain elements of which we are unaware, but which exert influence on our thoughts and behaviors. Some elements of the unconscious may have originally been conscious, say a traumatic event in childhood, but they have often been repressed—a process of pushing ideas into the unconscious. Discussion of the unconscious leads to Freud's famous three part division of the mind: 1) *id*, instinctual drives that seek immediate satisfaction according to the pleasure principle; 2) *ego*, conscious mental states governed by a reality principle; and 3) *superego*, the conscience which confronts the ego with moral rules, guilt and anxiety. The ego tries to reconcile the conflicting demands of the id—I want candy—and the superego—you shouldn't steal candy.

The *third* main idea in Freud was his focus on drives or instincts. These drives can manifest themselves in multiple ways. Freud, following the mechanical models of his day, felt these drives need to be discharged or pressure builds up. (This model is still influential, although it may not be accurate.) Freud emphasized the sexual drive to a much greater extent than any previous thinker, but other important drives include the drive for self-preservation and other life-enhancing drives (eros), as well as self-destructive drives for sadism, aggression and the death instinct (thanatos). However, Freud acknowledged that these thoughts were preliminary.

The *fourth* major aspect of Freud's theorizing was his offering of a developmental account of human personalities. He placed particular emphasis on the crucial importance of childhood for future psychological development. (Be nice to your children.) In fact, he didn't believe we could understand adults without knowing about their childhoods, including various sexual stages of development. While Freud has been criticized for his focus on the Oedipus complex, he was simply making the point that in the love between parents and children, the origin of adult love is first discovered. However, if individuals don't develop properly, then psychoanalysis may be the only way we can reverse the damage of childhood.

The Problem

Freud believed that well-being and mental harmony depend upon a harmonious relationship between various parts of the individual mind, and between a person and society. The ego seeks to satisfy its demands, but if there is a dearth of opportunities to do this, we experience pain and frustration. Yet even in the best of situations there is obsession, neuroticism, and other mental illness.

Freud also believed that repression caused neuroticism. For example, if someone has desires or beliefs that conflict with norms they are supposed to adhere to, then such feelings are often repressed. This is a defense mechanism used to avoid mental conflict. But repression ultimately doesn't work, for the desires and beliefs remain in the unconscious exerting their influence. They may lead to irrational, uncontrollable behaviors. Freud blamed a lot of neuroses on the social world, speculating that entire societies can be neurotic.

The Solution

Freud hoped that science could diagnose and improve human psychic problems. He wanted to restore a balance between parts of the mind, as well as between individuals and the social world. Freud concentrated on individuals—social reformers work on the societal reform—but he recognized the limits of working only with patients. Freud's method was to get his patients talking uninhibitedly about their past. When patients stopped talking,

Freud believed he was close to some unconsciously repressed memory or idea. He thought that by bringing this material to the awareness of the conscious mind, one could defeat these harmful thoughts.

Freud realized this process could take years, but he thought that psychotherapy could eventually bring greater harmony for individuals. Such therapy brings self-knowledge and, armed with that knowledge, patients may: a) replace repression of instinctual desires with rational self-control; b) divert instincts into acceptable behaviors; or c) even satisfy their desires. By bringing passions to the surface, Freud thought, one conquers them. He also thought that psychoanalysis could probably be applied to entire societies, since entire societies—say those unconcerned with the happiness of their citizens—are neurotic.

Freud as Scientist

Is psychoanalytic theory effective? Is it scientific? It is hard to judge the effectiveness of psychoanalysis for many reasons. *First,* understanding the causes of maladaptive behavior or thought—like abuse in childhood—doesn't imply that we can change them, some things may be impossible to undo, and we may have to accept or control them as best we can. *Second,* even if psychoanalysis works, it might be misapplied in practice. *Third,* what constitutes a cure resulting from psychoanalysis is vague. *Fourth,* how can we compare different neurotic patients, or establish control groups to compare them to? Generally we rely on anecdotal evidence about the effectiveness of therapy, which is by definition not scientific.

Testability is fundamental for a theory to have scientific status, so we must also ask whether these theories are testable. Unfortunately it isn't clear if Freud's theories are testable. Can we test the idea that the cause of a dream is a wish? Can we test that the unconscious is the cause of a slip of the tongue, a Freudian slip?

Now consider the idea of unconscious mental states. Do they explain or predict human behavior? If not, they're not scientific. In fact, attributing unconscious states to explain thoughts and behaviors is just a kind of "folk" psychology. Moreover, Freud did more than just postulate unconscious states; he said the process of repression pushes thoughts into the unconscious. But what does this repressing? Is this another consciousness? Is there a consciousness within a consciousness?

As for Freudian drives, how many there are? How are they to be distinguished from one another? How do we know that some drive, say a sexual one, is behind different behaviors, say artistic expression? We can sometimes be self-destructive, but does this imply we have a death instinct?

Defenders reply that psychoanalytic theory is not so much a scientific hypotheses as a *hermeneutic*, a way to understand the meaning of people's actions, words, dreams, neuroses, etc. We shouldn't criticize it for being less precise than physics or chemistry. People are complicated, interpreting them is more art than science, and a good psychotherapist understands human motivation better than most. Still, in the end, it isn't clear that Freud's theories are scientific.

Freud as Moralist

Bodily needs don't drive all human behavior, but Freud thought that our behavior shows we mostly operate according to "the pleasure principle." We generally seek satisfaction of our impulses, making us seem like non-human animals despite the fact that we derive satisfaction from, for example, the intellectual and artistic. Freud replied that these "satisfactions are mild" compared to eating, drinking, and sex. Moreover, he argued, the higher satisfactions are available only to those with rare gifts. But this doesn't seem right. What of the satisfaction of friendship, parenting, and music which are reliable and lasting forms of satisfaction? Perhaps Freud's views were colored by the physical pain he endured, and the world war through which he lived.

Freud didn't offer an overly optimistic view of reality. He saw religious belief as a projection of our childhood attitudes to our parents; we would like to believe that a Heavenly Father exists, is good, and watches out for us. Freud thought religion appealed to the emotions, not to reason. He also thought that religion could be understood as wish-fulfillment; we believe in things like immortality because we wish we were immortal.

In the end, Freud revolutionized our thinking by emphasizing how the unconscious and irrational drive us. Before Freud most thinkers didn't consider this.

Darwin: Humans Are Biological

Part I: Darwin and his Contemporaries

Before Darwin (1809 – 1882), scientists in the eighteenth and nineteenth centuries realized the world was much older than the Judeo-Christian tradition had assumed. The geologist Charles Lyell realized that layers of rock and soil were formed by the processes of eruption, sedimentation, and erosion over vast periods of time. Other scientists had discovered fossils of creatures that no longer existed. And others, including Darwin's grandfather Erasmus Darwin, had realized that the currently existing organisms evolved from predecessors through a series of small changes. Even some pre-Socratic thinkers had theories of evolution. The idea of evolution was in the air when Darwin was born.

Darwin on Natural Selection

Still, it is one thing to realize that something happened, but quite another to show *how* it had happened. What Darwin realized was

73

that natural selection was the mechanism of evolution. The most prominent theory about how this had happened before Darwin was Lamarck's theory. Lamarck believed in the "inheritance of acquired characteristics." If animals, for example, stretch their necks they might pass on long necks to their offspring. But Darwin soon realized that this was wrong.

While he came to Cambridge to study first medicine and then theology, he soon found himself fascinated with biology and geology—which led to a position as naturalist aboard the HMS Beagle on its five-year trip around the world. During his excursion he found bones of huge, extinct animals, the fossilized remains of sea creatures, an earthquake in Chile that uplifted earth, and other evidence of the processes of geological change. And he saw exotic the birds and other animals. The most noteworthy of which he found on the Galapagos Islands. The animals there were similar to those of the mainland, but differed slightly from one island to another. Even the beaks of little finches differed between islands, in each case in such a way as to help them get food on that island.

Shortly after his return to England he came up with the idea of natural selection, but he didn't publish the idea for almost twenty years. Not only were his ideas controversial, but evidently he didn't want to upset his wife Emma. Finally, after Alfred Wallace had arrived at the same conclusions, his friends encouraged him to publish his findings so that he could get the credit.

The idea of evolution can be logically deduced from four basic empirical facts:

1. Variation of traits exists among individuals in a given species;

2. Traits of parents are passed on to offspring;

You can easily see both of the above by looking around you—people look different, but they look more like their parents than they do other people's parent. Consider how we have bred animals and plants for thousands of years. If you want to produce a horse, you breed horses; if you want to produce a fast horse, you breed fast horses.) And just like humans artificially select to modify species—hence all those different dogs walking around—nature selects. That is called natural selection. Here are the other two facts:

3. The population of a species can increase quickly, and

4. An environment's resources typically can't support such increases.

Fact #3 can be confirmed when you realize that any pair of organisms can produce more than two offspring, in some cases thousands of offspring. Along with fact #4, this means that only a small portion of offspring reach maturity and reproduce, and thus there is competition to survive and reproduce. Given fact #1, we can infer that differences between individuals provide advantages in the battle to survive and reproduce. The traits of those that survive will be passed on, which means that the characteristic of populations gradually change and, given enough time, lead to new species. (Darwin also recognized sexual selection, the process of selecting for traits that help individuals reproduce—color of birds, antlers of the stag, or a peacock's tail.) The *Origin of Species* is basically seven hundred pages of evidence to support his logical inference—evidence from selective breeding, natural history, paleontology, and more.

Darwin on Human Evolution

While others immediately saw the implications of his theory for human bodies, Darwin waited another twelve years to publish the book that would make this case, *The Descent of Man.* In it he used anatomical, medical, embryological, and behavioral evidence to support the thesis that the human body has a common ancestry with other animals. *Today biological evolution is acknowledged as a fact beyond any reasonable doubt by biologists.* The overwhelming evidence for it comes from literally dozens of sciences including but not limited to: comparative anatomy, botany, embryology, biochemistry, genetics, anthropology, geology, molecular biology, chemistry, mathematics, population ecology, zoology, and more.

In fact, evolution is as well established scientifically as that gravity or atoms exist. Anyone who tells you differently is either: a) lying; or b) scientifically illiterate. The only way it might be false is if intelligent aliens or deceptive superintelligences or gods are playing tricks with our minds! (To confirm these claims visit the website of the National Academy of Sciences or any of the hundreds of scientific websites. Even better, major in biology at a good university, and you can learn to understand this fact first hand.)

Social Darwinism

But what are the social and ethical implications of the theory? Can a scientific fact say anything about values? Can you get an ought from an is? It seems not. For example, it may be a scientific fact that penicillin cures certain bacterial infections, but that doesn't mean that you ought to take penicillin. You only ought to take medicine if you value health. Or it may be a fact that large amounts of energy are released when we split atoms, but that doesn't imply that you ought to split them. So the fact of evolution doesn't seem to tell us what we ought to do.

But others disagree. Defenders of social Darwinism say that since evolution implies the most biologically fit survive, and since

76

biological success is a kind of ultimate value, those who survive must be the most valuable. They take Darwinism to imply that we survival matters most, that greed is good, and that selfishness is a virtue. In other words, those who survive are not only the most biologically fit, but the fittest in a larger sense.

In the USA today this is generally taken to mean those with the most money. Not surprisingly Ayn Rand, the matron of today's Republican Party in the USA, titled her work on ethics: *The Virtue of Selfishness*. It argues that selfishness is a moral virtue. This type of thinking implies that charity, health-care, social security, public education, child care, and more are pointless. You should let the inferior (poor or middle class) die; they are not as valuable as the idle rich. Many thinkers in the USA in the nineteenth-century adopted this attitude, and it was as common among the robber barons at that time as it is among large elements of today's Republican Party in America. It advocates competition to weed out what Ayn Rand, and Republican politicians call moochers. (So strange given that the wealthy are generally the welfare beneficiaries of society's largess.)

It is but a small step from social Darwinism to racism and genocide. But it doesn't follow that those who are biologically fit—like cockroaches—are morally, artistically, intellectually, spiritually, or psychologically fit. Those who have the most children or the most money aren't necessarily the best either. But then social Darwinism was not Darwin's idea, nor did he subscribe to it. The idea came from the philosopher Herbert Spencer, and was embraced by many of the wealthy in America in the nineteenth century, as it still is today. How ironic that so many of the opponents of biological Darwinism in the American political arena today are supporters of social Darwinism. They disbelieve what we know to be true, and believe what it almost certainly both false and immoral.

Darwin's Own Values

Darwin suggested that not only had human bodies evolved from lower forms, but so too had our intelligence, language, emotions, morality and religion. Darwin knew it was speculative to extend evolution from human bodies to their minds and behaviors, but today we know that he was right about all this. Nonetheless, some of his ideas, especially about selection operating at the level of the group—group selection—are matters of controversy today. (Yes there are controversies about *how* evolution happened, but none about *that* it happened.) He also realized that culture as well as biology influence ethical values and religious beliefs.

The reply to the social Darwinists points out that evolution has given us sympathy for our fellows, and the intelligence to make a just and moral world. This is every bit as natural as a survival of the fittest. Darwin himself believed that human sympathy and compassion were noble and natural. But in the end the appeal to the ethics of Kant, Marx, or Christianity at its best goes beyond any biological imperative.

As for religion, much has been said about Darwin's religious beliefs. Yet the truth is that by the end of his life, he was almost certainly a closet atheist. He had come a long way from preparing for the clergy as a young man, but by all accounts he was a humble man, dedicated father, and affectionate husband.

Part II: The Reaction Against Biological Accounts of Human Nature:

The Genetic Basis of Heredity

Darwin knew that there are variations between individuals, and that these variations are inherited, but he didn't know the mechanism of inheritance. This mechanism was discovered by Gregor Mendel (1822 – 1884) who figured out that distinct casual factors—what we call genes—are passed from parents to offspring. We now know that sometimes genes change or mutate randomly, and that accounts for genetic variation. Putting Mendelian genetics together with Darwinian natural selection, along with precise mathematically modeling, resulted in the "modern synthesis." This feat, accomplished during the 1930s and 1940s, is considered one of the great scientific achievements of all time. To further solidify the truth of evolution, the biochemical basis of gene copying was uncovered with the discovery of DNA in 1953 by Crick and Watson. This ushered in the era of molecular biology. Today we understand evolution at a molecular level that Darwin could only imagine. Today, in laboratories around the world, biological evolution is confirmed every single day. Over and over and over; day after day after day!

Eugenics, Racism, and Sexism

Many were led to the conclusion that evolution implied that there are innate differences between individuals, sexes, or races. Perhaps this implies that we should let the physically or mentally weak die, or at least keep them from breeding. This led to the idea of eugenics, the study of how to produce fit offspring. In the early twentieth century much of the western world was enamored with this idea. Yet even if this is ethically acceptable, it is practically impossible to know who has "bad" genes. Moreover such judgments, as Darwin himself realized, were sociological not biological. For example, different races are all the same species. Racism and sexism emanate from prejudice against groups without biological justification. Race is not even a justifiable biological concept. More genetic diversity exists within populations than between them.

Intelligence Tests, Sociology, and Anthropology

Many went further to suggest that woman and some racial groups were intellectually inferior to white men, which raises a number of questions. Is there some single thing called intelligence that can be measured? Even if there were such a thing, how would it be measured? Are there different kinds of intelligence, say social or moral intelligence as compared to simply being good at math or language? If we have tests to measure this supposed intelligence, how do we know if the results are due to innate ability or social opportunities? Today, the whole idea of intelligence measurement is controversial.

Moreover, the burgeoning social sciences of the nineteenth century emphasized the influence of culture rather than biology to explain human behavior. Social scientists generally say that facts about human beings are: 1) physical; 2) psychological; and 3) social/cultural. Most importantly, social facts aren't reducible to biology, and the social world strongly affects the individual. For example, if you were raised in a non-English speaking culture, you would probably not have learned English.

Behaviorist Psychology

There was also a reaction against supposedly Darwinian ideas in psychology, especially the idea of instincts. To make psychology more scientific, John B. Watson (1878-1958) proposed that psychology study observable behaviors and reject the appeal to vague notions like instincts, intentions, or other mental states. He was adamant about environmental influence, thinking that he could make any healthy child a world-class scholar, musician, or athlete given the right environment. This program was continued by B.F. Skinner (1904 - 1990) at Harvard. He argued that the environment selects behaviors by rewarding them, or eliminates behaviors by punishing them—by classical and operate conditioning. In other words, behavior is mostly explained by environmental causes. While there is some truth to this, studies of identical twins reared apart—such twins share identical genomes—reveal the strong influence of biological on behavior.

Because of the perversions of social Darwinism, racism, sexism and other immoral ideas attached to Darwinism, the biology of human nature was ignored until the 1960s. And while we acknowledge the horrors of racism, sexism and social Darwinism, we shouldn't ignore facts about our biology. A new wave of thinkers have now rediscovered and extended the Darwinian paradigm. They have brought about a scientific revolution. We now turn to these ideas.

Part III: The Return of Human Nature

Genes and Memes

Throughout the 1960s and 1970s evolutionary theory was further confirmed and understood at greater depths. Mathematical insights shed light on adaptation, kin selection (altruism toward close relatives), reciprocal altruism (directed toward other species), and the relevance of game theory to evolving populations (non-human animals often find themselves in situations with the structure of a prisoner's dilemma.) This allowed evolution to be understood at the level of the gene, an idea popularized by the evolutionary biologist Richard Dawkins in his book, *The Selfish Gene*. The title of the book helps us see evolution in terms of the competition between genes. With today's mathematical modeling, we can see this in great detail.

At the end of the book Dawkins argued that culture evolves analogously to biology only much faster. The elements of culture are ideas, beliefs, practices, fashions, etc. which he called *memes*. Some memes catch on and survive—say a belief in immortality, or wings for aircraft—while others go extinct—like the idea of celibacy for everyone, or wings attached to your arms. Memes are transferred from one mind to another, rather than being transferred from one body to another like genes. Thus you can spread memes much faster than you can spread genes. Cultural evolution is fast while biological evolution is slow. Cultural evolution is also guided by Lamarckian "inheritance of acquired characteristics." You inherit your religious or sports team loyalties from your parents or friends. Christianity or a love of Manchester United is not in the genes.

The Rise of Ethology

In the mid-twentieth century a new discipline arose, ethology, which studies animal behavior in its natural environment. Its key finding was that behavior is hard-wired as physiology. Many behaviors in animals can't be explained by environmental conditioning; they are clearly hard-wired or innate. They exist independent of experience or learning, they are fixed. It seems evolution has designed species-wide behaviors.

Konrad Lorenz (1903 -1989) became famous for studying animal behavior, especially the imprinting of ducks to the first moving thing they see. He assumed imprinting was an innate feature of many animals, but he reached this conclusion too quickly. For how do we know which traits are learned and which are innate? Moreover, if they are innate, then they seem unable to be eradicated if they are anti-social. Lorenz also believed in group selection, but as we have seen the level at which selection operates is still open to debate.

Chomsky and Cognitive Psychology

While B.F. Skinner thought that language could be explained by the social environment, the linguist Noam Chomsky (1928 -)

showed that human facility with language is different from other animal behaviors. (Chomsky is one of the most important linguists in history, although today he is known mostly as a political philosopher critical of American domestic and foreign policy.) All normal humans can learn language, and no animal language approaches the complexity of human language. Even chimps that use sign language fall far short of human language. Chomsky famously argued that the speed at which infants learn language and grammatical suggested that this capacity is innate. Thus he concluded there is a kind of universal human grammar that is a result of our evolutionary history. This has been the most influential idea in twentieth century linguistics. It implies that our ability with language is an evolutionary adaptation; language aids survival. Today research on this topic is pursued by linguists, neuroscientists, and evolutionary biologists. But if language has a strong evolutionary component, then wouldn't other human behaviors be influenced similarly?

E. O. Wilson and Sociobiology

The Harvard biologist E. O. Wilson (1929 -) was the first to argue convincingly that the humanities and social sciences can be reduced to biology. This project, if successful, will lead to the new science of sociobiology. In his Pulitzer Prize-winning book, *On Human Nature*, Wilson offered biological explanations for human social behaviors like aggression, sex, ethics, and religion. Needless to say Wilson's ideas have provoked controversy, especially from social scientists who don't want to believe their disciplines can be biologized. Moreover, they fear that Wilson's views give support to racist or sexist views. Even some biologists believe he is underestimating the influence of culture. Wilson, a grey-haired grandfather, even had a bucket of water dumped on his head at a conference to protest what some see as the implications of his views!

But Wilson's detractors were wrong. He clearly saw that both biology and culture as influential on human nature, and he made this clear to anyone who has read him carefully. In fact, he wrote an entire book on gene-culture co-evolution. Yet he did say that, for the moment, "genes hold culture on a leash." We are not that far removed from our evolutionary past; its imprint is apparent in our behaviors. I think he's right.

The Integrated Causal Model

What Wilson called sociobiology is today called evolutionary psychology. This is the same thing, but with fewer negative connotations. This school of thought applies Darwinian insights to the human mind and human behaviors. Its key premises are: 1) universal human nature refers primarily to evolved psychological mechanisms; 2) these mechanisms are adaptations selected for over many generations that help us survive and reproduce, (remember though what was formerly adaptive and what is now adapted can be different—going to college may now be adaptive, aggression may no longer be); 3) our minds contain adaptations from distant ancestors, all the way back to the Pleistocene. This final point has been challenged by evidence that genes may evolve faster than previously thought.

The contemporary researchers Cosmides and Tooby also critique the standard social science emphasis on the environmental factors, advancing what they call the integrated causal model. They argue that because social scientists fear racist and sexist ideologies, these scientists have been blind to the overwhelming evidence for evolutionarily produced cognitive mechanisms. Like Wilson, Cosmides and Tooby propose that a complex web of causal factors produced human nature. Behind any human phenomena is: 1) natural selection operating over eons of time producing innate cognitive structures; 2) historical development; 3) unique genes as the result of sexual reproduction; 4) physical, cultural, and social environments; and 5) information processing which leads to beliefs and desires.

What all this means is that there are innate mental modules resulting from natural selection that operated on our distant ancestors, especially regarding factors relevant to reproductive fitness like perception, language, cooperation, mate selection, parental care. Still this is all open to further investigation. There is much more to be learned.

Darwin's Words

We'll end this section by letting Darwin speak for himself. As for human nature, Darwin was a scientific realist unafraid of the truth:

[Humans in their] arrogance think [themselves] a great work worthy the interposition of a deity. More humble and I think truer to consider [them] created from animals.

And he knew that the truth would be illuminating. As he wrote in his Notebooks:

He who understand [the] baboon would do more toward metaphysics than Locke. Plato says that our 'imaginary ideas' arise from the preexistence of the soul, [they] are not derivable from experience—read monkeys for preexistence.

Yet at the same time he was an artist who saw beauty in the truth:

There is grandeur in this view of life, with its several powers, having been originally breathed into a few forms or into one; and that, whilst this planet has gone cycling on according to the fixed law of gravity, from so simple a beginning endless forms most beautiful and most wonderful have been, and are being, evolved.

Chapter 4 – Do We Have to Die?

This is the terror: to have emerged from nothing, to have a name, consciousness of self, deep inner feelings, an excruciating inner yearning for life and self-expression—and with all this yet to die.
~ Ernest Becker

Is There An Afterlife?

The literature on death is voluminous and deserving of its own book length study. What we can do here is briefly discuss a few of the issues involved. Belief in immorality is widespread, as anthropological studies reveal, but most people regard death as the ultimate tragedy and crave continued existence. Yet there is little if any evidence for immortality; and we do not personally know anyone who came back from the dead to tell us about an afterlife. Still, many people cling to any indirect evidence they can—near death experiences, belief in reincarnation, ghost stories, communication with the dead, and the like. The problem is that none of this so-called evidence stands up well to critical scrutiny. It is so much more likely that the propensity of individuals to deceive or be deceived explains such beliefs, than that these phenomena are real. Those who accept such evidence are most likely grasping at straws—engaging in wishful thinking.

Modern science generally ignores this so-called evidence for an afterlife for a number of reasons. First, the soul which is thought immortal plays no explanatory or predictive role in the modern scientific study of human beings. Second, overwhelming evidence supports the view that consciousness ceases when brain functioning does. If ghosts or disembodied spirits exist, then we would be forced to rethink much of modern science—such as the belief that consciousness cannot exist without matter!

Of course this cursory treatment of the issue does not establish that an afterlife is impossible, especially since that possibility depends on answers to complicated philosophical questions about personal identity and the mind-body problem. But suffice it to say that explaining either the dualistic theory of life after death— where the soul separates from the body at death and lives forever—or the monist theory—where a new glorified body related to the earthly body lives on forever—is extraordinarily difficult. In the first case substance dualism must be defended, and in the second case the miraculous idea of the new body must be explained. Either way the philosophical task is enormous. Clearly the scientific winds are blowing against these ancient beliefs.

Given these considerations, we will proceed as if death is the end of human existence; we will advance without philosophically problematic assumptions about the existence of an afterlife. This has the advantage that if we find meaning without introducing such assumptions, we will be more assured of our results. And if it miraculously turns out that when we die we really do move to a better neighborhood … so much the better.

Is Death Bad For Us?

Vincent Barry, professor emeritus at Bakersfield College, carefully considered this question in his 2007 textbook, *Philosophical Thinking About Death and Dying*. I reconstruct his discussion in what follows.

Is Death Bad? – One of Barry's main concerns is whether death is or isn't bad for us. As he notes, the argument that death isn't bad derives from Epicurus' aphorism: "When I am, death isn't; and when death is, I am not." Epicurus taught that fear in general, and fear of the gods and death in particular, was evil.

Consequently, using reason to rid ourselves of these fears was a primary goal of his speculative thinking. A basic assumptions of his thought was a materialistic psychology in which mind was composed of atoms, and death the dispersal of those atoms. Thus death isn't then bad for us since something can be bad only if we are affected by it; but we have no sensation after death and thus being dead can't be bad for us. Note that this doesn't imply that the process or the prospect of dying can't be bad for us—they can— nor does Epicurus deny that we might prefer life to death. His argument is that being dead isn't bad for the one who has died.

Epicurus' argument relies on two separate assumptions—the experience requirement and the existence requirement. The *experience requirement* states roughly:

1) Harm to someone is bad for them. For something to be bad for someone it must be experienced by them.

2) Death is a state of no experience.

3) Therefore death can't be bad for someone.

The *existence requirement* can be summarized thus:

1) A person can be harmed only if they exist.

2) A dead person doesn't exist.

3) Therefore a dead person can't be harmed.

As we will see, counter arguments attack one of the two requirements. Either they try to show that someone can be harmed without experiencing the harm, or that someone who is dead can still be harmed.

One noted philosopher who attacks the Epicurean view is Thomas Nagel. In his essay "Death," Nagel argues that death is bad for someone who dies even if that person doesn't consciously survive death. According to this deprivation theory, death is bad for persons who die because of the good things their deaths deprive them of. However, if death is bad because it limits the possibility of future goods, is death not then good in limiting the possibility of future evils? So the possibility of future goods doesn't by itself show that death is bad; to show that one would have to show that a future life would be worth living, that is, that it would contain more good than bad. But how can any deprivation theory explain how it's bad for us to be deprived of something if we don't experience that deprivation? How can what we don't know hurt us?

In reply Nagel argues that we can be harmed without being aware of it. An intelligent man reduced to the state of infancy by a brain injury has suffered a great misfortune, even if unaware of, and contented in, his injurious state. Nagel argues that many states that we don't experience can be bad for us—the betrayal of a friend, the loss of reputation, or the unfaithfulness of a spouse. And just as an adult reduced to infancy is the subject of a misfortune, so too is one who is dead. But critics wonder who it's that is the subject of this harm? Even if it's bad to be deprived of certain goods, who is it that is deprived? How can the dead be harmed? There apparently is no answer to this question.

And there is another problem. While the deprivation argument may explain why death is bad for us, it follows from it that being denied prenatal existence would also be bad. Yet we don't ordinarily consider ourselves harmed by not having been born sooner. How can we explain this asymmetry?

Epicurus argued that this asymmetry couldn't be explained, and we should feel indifferent to death just as we do to prenatal existence. This sentiment was echoed by Mark Twain:

> Annihilation has no terrors for me, because I have already tried it before I was born—a hundred million years—and I

have suffered more in an hour, in this life, than I remember to have suffered in the whole hundred million years put together. There was a peace, a serenity, an absence of all sense of responsibility, an absence of worry, an absence of care, grief, perplexity; and the presence of a deep content and unbroken satisfaction in that hundred million years of holiday which I look back upon with a tender longing and with a grateful desire to resume when the opportunity comes.

In reply the deprivationists argue that we don't have to hold symmetrical views about prenatal and postnatal experience—claiming instead that asymmetrical views are consistent with ordinary experience. To see why consider the following. Would you rather have suffered a long surgical operation last year or undergo a short one tomorrow? Would you rather have had pleasure yesterday, or pleasure tomorrow? In both cases we have more concern with the future than the past; we are less interested in past events than in future ones. Death in the future deprives us of future goods, whereas prenatal nonexistence deprived us of past goods about which we are now indifferent. For all these reason Barry concludes that death is probably bad and a fear of it is rational.

Given that death is probably bad for us, what then do we do, assuming death is inevitable? Perhaps we should just be optimistic. We really haven't anything to lose by being optimistic and, given the current reality of death, this is a wise option. William James suggested as much in his essay "The Will to Believe,"

> We stand on a mountain pass in the midst of whirling snow and blinding mist, through which we get glimpses now and then of paths which may be deceptive. If we stand still we shall be frozen to death. If we take the wrong road we shall

91

be dashed to pieces. We don't certainly know whether there
is any right one. What must we do? 'Be strong and of a
good courage.' Act for the best, hope for the best, and take
what comes. ... If death ends all, we can't meet death
better.

But even such stirring words don't change the fact that death is
bad. Bad because it puts an end to something which at its best is
beautiful; bad because all the knowledge and insight and wisdom
of that person is lost; bad because of the harm it does to the living;
bad because it causes people to be unconcerned about the future
beyond their short lifespan; and bad because we know in our
bones, that if we had the choice, and if our lives were going well,
we would choose to on. That death is generally bad—especially so
for the physically, morally, and intellectually vigorous—is nearly
self-evident.

But most of all, death is bad because it renders completely
meaningful lives impossible. It's true that longer lives don't
guarantee meaningful ones, but all other things being equal, longer
lives contain the possibility of more meaning than shorter ones.
(Both the quality and the quantity of a life are relevant to its
meaning; both are necessary though not sufficient conditions for
meaning.) An infinite life can be without meaning, but a life of no
duration, a non-existent life, is by definition meaningless. A happy,
healthy, well-lived finite life of twenty years may contain a lot of
meaning, but an identically well-lived life would be more
meaningful if it were lived for another twenty or forty or eighty or
ten-thousand years. While there are no guarantees, the possibility
of greater meaning–the total meaning of a life–increases
proportionately with the length of a lifetime.

Yes, there are indeed fates worse than death, and in some
circumstances death may be welcomed even if it extinguishes the

further possibility of meaning. Nevertheless, death is one of the worst fates that can befall us, despite the consolations offered by the deathists—the lovers of death. We may become bored with eternal consciousness, but as long as we can end our lives if we want, as long as we can opt out of immortality, who wouldn't want the option to live forever?

Only if we can choose whether to live or die are we really free. Our lives aren't our own if they can be taken from us without our consent, and, to the extent death can be delayed or prevented, further possibilities for meaning ensue. Perhaps with our hard-earned knowledge we can slay death, thereby opening up the possibility for more meaningful lives. This is perhaps the fundamental imperative for our species. For now the best we can do is to remain optimistic in the face of the great tragedy that is death.

How Science May Defeat Death

If death is our end, then all we can do is die and hope for the best. But perhaps we don't have to die. Many scientists now believe that humans can overcome death and achieve immortality through the use of future technologies. But how will we do this?

The first way we might achieve physical immortality is by conquering our biological limitations—we age, become diseased, and suffer trauma. Aging research, while woefully underfunded, has yielded positive results. Average life expectancies have tripled since ancient times, increasing by more than fifty percent in the industrial world in the last hundred years, and most scientists think we will continue to extend our life-spans. We know that some jellyfish and bacteria are essentially immortal, and the bristlecone pine may be too. There is no thermodynamic necessity for senescence—aging is a presumed byproduct of evolution — although why mortality was selected for remains a mystery. Yet some scientists believe we can conquer aging altogether—in the next few decades with sufficient investment—most notably the Cambridge researcher Aubrey de Grey.

If we do unlock the secrets of aging, we will simultaneously defeat other diseases as well, since many of them are symptoms of aging. Many researchers now consider aging itself to be a disease which progresses as you age. There are a number of strategies that could render disease mostly inconsequential. Nanotechnology may give us nanobot cell-repair machines and robotic blood cells; biotechnology may supply replacement tissues and organs; genetics may offer genetic medicine and engineering; and full-fledge genetic engineering could make us impervious to disease.

Trauma is a more intransigent problem from the biological perspective, although it too could be defeated through some combination of cloning, regenerative medicine, and genetic engineering. We can even imagine that your physicality could be recreated from a bit of your DNA, and other technologies could then fast forward your regenerated body to the age of your traumatic death, where a backup file containing your experiences and memories would be implanted in your brain. Even the dead may be resuscitated if they have undergone the process of cryonics—preserving organisms at very low temperatures in glass-like states. Ideally these clinically dead would be brought back to life when technology is sufficiently advanced. This may now be science fiction, but if nanotechnology fulfills its promise, there is a good chance that cryonics will succeed.

In addition to biological strategies for eliminating death, there are a number of technological scenarios for immortality which utilize advanced brain scanning techniques, artificial intelligence, and robotics. The most prominent scenarios have been advanced by the futurist Ray Kurzweil, who argues that the exponential growth of computing power, combined with advances in other technologies, will make it possible to upload the contents of one's consciousness into a virtual reality. This could be accomplished by cybernetics, whereby hardware would be gradually installed in the brain until the entire brain was running on that hardware, or via scanning the brain and simulating or transferring its contents to a sufficiently advanced computer. Either way we would no longer be living in a physical world.

In fact we may already be living in a computer simulation. The Oxford philosopher and futurist Nick Bostrom argues that advanced civilizations may have created computer simulations containing individuals with artificial intelligence and we might unknowingly be in such a simulation. Bostrom concludes that one of the following must be the case: civilizations never have the technology to run simulations; they have the technology but decided not to use it; or we almost certainly live in a simulation.

If we don't like the idea of being immortal in a virtual reality—or we don't like the idea that we may already be in one—we could upload our brain to a genetically engineered body if we like the feel of flesh, or to a robotic body if we like the feel of silicon or whatever materials comprised the robotic body. Along these lines MIT's Rodney Brooks envisions the merger of human flesh and machines, whereby humans slowly incorporate technology into their bodies, thus becoming more machine-like and indestructible. So a cyborg future may await us.

An evolutionary perspective underlies all these speculative scenarios. Once we embrace that perspective, it's easy to imagine that *our descendants will resemble us about as much as we do the amino acids from which we sprang.* Our knowledge is growing exponentially and, given eons of time for future innovation, it's easy to envisage that humans will defeat death and evolve in unimaginable ways. Remember that our evolution is no longer moved by the painstakingly slow process of Darwinian evolution—where bodies exchange information through genes—but by cultural evolution—where brains exchange information through memes. The most prominent feature of cultural evolution is the exponentially increasing pace of technological evolution—an evolution that may soon culminate in a *technological singularity*.

The technological singularity, an idea first proposed by the mathematician Vernor Vinge, refers to the hypothetical future emergence of greater than human intelligence. Since the capabilities of such intelligences are difficult for our minds to comprehend, the singularity is seen as an event horizon beyond which the future becomes impossible to understand or predict. Nevertheless, we may surmise that this intelligence explosion will lead to increasingly powerful minds that will solve the problem of death.

But why conquer death? Why is death bad? It's bad because it ends something which at its best is good; because it puts an end to our projects; because the wisdom and knowledge of a person is lost at death; because it harms the living; because it causes apathy about the future beyond our short life-span; because it renders fully meaningful lives impossible; and because we know that if we had the choice, and if our lives were going well, we would choose to live on. That death is generally bad—especially for the physically and intellectually vigorous—is nearly self-evident.

Yes, there are indeed fates worse than death, and in some circumstances death may be welcomed. Nevertheless for most of us most of the time, death is one of the worst fates that can befall us. That is why we think that suicide and murder and starvation and cancer are bad things. That is why we cry at funerals.

Death Should Be Optional

Today there are serious thinkers—Ray Kurzweil, Hans Moravec, Michio Kaku, Marshall Brain, Aubrey de Grey, Elon Musk, Stephen Hawking and others—who foresee that technology may enable humans to defeat death. There are also dissenters who argue that this is exceedingly unlikely. And there are those like Bill Joy who think that such technologies are technologically feasible but morally reprehensible.

As a non-scientist I am not qualified to evaluate scientific claims about what science can and can't do. What I can say is that plausible scenarios for overcoming death have now appeared. This leads to the following questions: If individuals could choose immortality, should they? Should societies fund and promote research to defeat death?

The question regarding individuals has a straightforward answer—we should respect the right of autonomous individuals to choose for themselves. If an effective pill that stops or reverses aging becomes available at your local pharmacy, then you should be free to use it. My guess is that such a pill would be wildly popular! (Consider what people spend on vitamins and other elixirs on the basis of little or no evidence of their efficacy.) Or if, as you approach death, you are offered the opportunity to have your consciousness transferred to your younger cloned body, a genetically engineered body, a robotic body, or into a virtual reality, you should be free to do so. I believe that nearly everyone will use such technologies once they are demonstrated effective. But if individuals prefer to die in the hope that the gods will revive them in a paradise, thereby granting them reprieve from everlasting torment, then we should respect that too. Individuals should be free to end their lives even after death has become optional for them.

Chapter 4 – Do We Have to Die?

The argument about whether a society should fund and promote the research relevant to eliminating death is more complex. Societies currently invest vast sums on entertainment rather than scientific research; although the latter is a clearly a better societal investment. Ultimately the arguments for and against immortality must speak for themselves, but we reiterate that once science and technology have extended life significantly, or defeated death altogether, the point will be moot. By then almost everyone will choose to live as long as possible. In fact many people do that now, at great cost, and often gaining only a few additional months of bad health. Imagine then how quickly they will choose life over death when the techniques are proven to lead to longer, healthier lives. As for the naysayers, they will get used to new technologies just like they did to previous ones.

Nonetheless the virtual inevitability of advanced technologies to extend life doesn't imply their desirability, and many thinkers have campaigned actively and vehemently against utilizing such options. The defenders of death advocate maintaining the status quo with its daily dose of 150,000 deaths worldwide. Prominent among such thinkers are Leon Kass, who chaired George W. Bush's Council on Bioethics from 2001-2005, Francis Fukuyama, a Senior Fellow at the Center on Democracy, Development and the Rule of Law at Stanford, and Bill McKibbon, the Schumann Distinguished Scholar at Middlebury College.

Kass opposes euthanasia, human cloning, and embryonic stem cell research and was an early opponent of in vitro fertilization, which he thought would obscure truths about human life and society. (IVF had none of the dire consequences that Kass predicted; today the technology now goes mostly unnoticed.) One of Kass' main concerns is with the enhancement capability of biotechnology, which he fears will become a substitute for traditional human virtues. His concerns about modifying our biological inheritance extend to his worries about life extension. He values the natural cycle of life and views death as a desirable end—mortality, he says, is a blessing in disguise.

Fukuyama argues that biotechnology will alter human nature beyond recognition with terrible consequences. One would be the undermining of liberal democracy due to radical inequality between those who had access to such technologies and those who didn't . (Although there is plenty of social and economic inequality around today.) At an even more fundamental level, Fukuyama worries that the consequences of modifying humans is unknown. Should human beings really want to control their very natures? Fukuyama argues that we should be humble about such matters or "we may unwittingly invite the transhumanists to deface humanity with their genetic bulldozers and psychotropic shopping malls.

McKibbon admits the allure of technological utopia, knowing that it will be hard to resist, but he fears that the richness of human life would be lost in a post-human world. Even if we were godlike, spending our time meditating on the meaning of the cosmos or reflecting on our own consciousness like Aristotle's god, McKibbon says he would not trade his life for such an existence. He wouldn't want to be godlike, preferring instead to smell the fragrant leaves, feel the cool breeze, and see the fall colors. Yes there is pain, suffering, cruelty, and death in the world, but this world is enough. "To call this world enough isn't to call it perfect or fair or complete or easy. But enough, just enough. And us in it."

There is a lot to say against all these views, but one wonders why these thinkers see human nature as sacrosanct. Is our nature so sacred that we should be apologists for it? Isn't it arrogant to think so highly of ourselves? This human nature produced what Hegel lampooned as "the slaughter-bench at which the happiness of peoples, the wisdom of States, and the virtue of individuals have been victimized." Surely we can do a better than what was created through genetic mutations and environmental selection.

Still we must concede something to these warnings. The same technologies that may make us immortal are also the ones that bring robotic police and unmanned planes. Yet there is no way to assure that we will not suffer a nightmarish future no matter how we proceed. There is no risk-free way to proceed. With greater knowledge comes greater power; and with greater power comes the possibility of making life better or worse. The future with all its promises and perils will come regardless—all we can do is do our best.

The defense of immortality against such attacks has been undertaken most thoroughly by the recent intellectual and cultural movement known as *transhumanism*, which affirms the possibility and desirability of using technology to eliminate aging and overcome all other human limitations. Adopting an evolutionary perspective, transhumanists maintain that humans are in a relatively early phase of their development. They agree with humanism—that human beings matter and that reason, freedom, and tolerance make the world better—but emphasizes that we can become more than human by changing ourselves. This involves employing high-tech methods to transform the species and direct our own evolution, as opposed to relying on biological evolution or low-tech methods like education and training.

If science and technology develop sufficiently, this would lead to a stage where humans would no longer be recognized as human, but better described as post-human. But why would people want to transcend human nature? Because

> they yearn to reach intellectual heights as far above any
> current human genius as humans are above other primates;
> to be resistant to disease and impervious to aging; to have

unlimited youth and vigor; to exercise control over their own desires, moods, and mental states; to be able to avoid feeling tired, hateful, or irritated about petty things; to have an increased capacity for pleasure, love, artistic appreciation, and serenity; to experience novel states of consciousness that current human brains can't access. It seems likely that the simple fact of living an indefinitely long, healthy, active life would take anyone to posthumanity if they went on accumulating memories, skills, and intelligence.

And why would one want these experiences to last forever? Transhumanists answer that they would like to do, think, feel, experience, mature, discover, create, enjoy, and love beyond what one can do in seventy or eighty years. All of us would benefit from the wisdom and love that come with time.

The conduct of life and the wisdom of the heart are based upon time; in the last quartets of Beethoven, the last words and works of 'old men' like Sophocles and Russell and Shaw, we see glimpses of a maturity and substance, an experience and understanding, a grace and a humanity, that isn't present in children or in teenagers. They attained it because they lived long; because they had time to experience and develop and reflect; time that we might all have. Imagine such individuals—a Benjamin Franklin, a Lincoln, a Newton, a Shakespeare, a Goethe, an Einstein—enriching our world not for a few decades but for centuries. Imagine a world made of such individuals. It would truly be what Arthur C. Clarke called "Childhood's End"—the beginning of the adulthood of humanity.

Chapter 4 – Do We Have to Die?

As for the charge that creating infinitely long life spans tamper with nature, remember that something isn't good or bad because it's natural. Some natural things are bad and some are good; some artificial things are bad and some are good. (Assuming we can even make an intelligible distinction between the natural and the unnatural.) As for the charge that long lives undermine humanity, the key is to be humane, and merely being human doesn't guarantee that you are humane. As for the claim that death is natural, again, that doesn't make it good. Moreover it was natural to die before the age of thirty for most of human history, so we live unnaturally long lives now by comparison. And few people complain about this. But even if death is natural, so too is the desire for immortality. Yes people had to accept death when it was inevitable, but now such acceptance impede progress in eradicating death. Death should be optional.

Additionally there are important reasons to be suspicious about the anti-immortality arguments—many are made by those who profit from death. For example if a church sells immortality its business model is threatened by a competitor offering the real thing. Persons no longer need to join an institution if its promise of immortality is actually delivered elsewhere for a comparable cost. Anti-technology arguments may be motivated by self-interest and, as we all know, most people hesitate to believe anything that is inconsistent with how they make money. Just look at the historical opposition to the rise of modern science and the accompanying real miracles it brought. Or to tobacco companies opposition to the evidence linking smoking with cancer, or to the oil companies opposition to the evidence linking burning fossil fuels with global climate change.

A connected reason to be suspicious of the defenders of death is that death is so interwoven into their world-view, that rejecting it would essentially destabilize that world-view, thereby undercutting their psychological stability. If one has invested a lifetime in a world-view in which dying and an afterlife are an integral part, a challenge to that world-view will almost always be rejected. The great American philosopher Charles Sanders Pierce captured this point perfectly:

> Doubt is an uneasy and dissatisfied state from which we struggle to free ourselves and pass into the state of belief; while the latter is a calm and satisfactory state which we don't wish to avoid, or to change to a belief in anything else. On the contrary, we cling tenaciously, not merely to believing, but to believing just what we do believe.

The defeat of death completely obliterates most world-views that have supported humans for millennia; no wonder it undermines psychological stability and arouses fierce opposition. Thus monetary and psychological reasons help to explain much opposition to life-extending therapies. Still people do change their minds. We now no longer accept dying at age thirty and think it a great tragedy when it happens; I argue that our descendents will feel similarly about our dying at eighty. Eighty years may be a relatively long lifespan compared with those of our ancestors, but it may be exceedingly brief when compared to those of our descendents. Our mind children may shed the robotic equivalent of tears at our short and painful lifespan, as we do for the short, difficult lives of our forbearers.

In the end death eradicates the possibility of complete meaning for individuals; surely that is reason enough to desire immortality for all conscious beings. Still, for those who don't want immortality, they should be free to die. But for those of us that long to live forever, we should free to do so. I want more freedom. I want death to be optional.

Chapter 5 – The Unimaginable Future

What Would Life Be Like Inside a Computer?

If science and technology defeat death, and if they overcome all other human limitations—psychological, intellectual, moral, physical—then our descendents may live in a world now unimaginable to us. They will resemble us about as much as we do the amino acids from which we sprang.

Of course I am in no position as a non-scientist to judge the feasibility of, for example, mind uploading; experts have both praised and pilloried its viability. Nor can I judge what it would be like to live within a virtual reality. In fact, I don't even know what it's like to be a dog or another person. And I don't know if I would have subjective experiences inside a computer, since we don't even know how the *brain* gives rise to subjective experiences. So I certainly don't know what it would be like to exist as a simulated mind inside a computer or a robotic body. What I do know is that the Oxford philosopher and futurist Nick Bostrom has argued that there is a good chance that we live in a simulation now. And if he's right, then you're having subjective experiences inside a computer simulation as you read this.

But does it make sense to think a mind program could run on something other than a brain? Isn't subjective consciousness rooted in the biological brain? Yes, for the moment our mental software runs on the brain's hardware. But there is no necessary reason that this has to be the case. If I told you a hundred years ago that integrated silicon circuits will someday play chess better than grandmasters, model future climate change, recognize faces and voices, and solve famous mathematical problems, you would be astonished. Today you might reply, "But computers still can't feel emotions or taste a strawberry." And you are right they can't—for now. But what about a thousand years from now? What about ten thousand or a million years from now? Do you really think that in a million years the best minds will run on carbon based brains?

If you still find it astounding that minds could run on silicon chips, consider how remarkable it's that our minds run on meat! Imagine beings from another planet with cybernetic brains discovering that human brains are made of meat. That we are conscious and communicate by means of our meat brains. *They* would be amazed. They would find this as implausible as many of us do the idea that minds could run on silicon.

The key to understanding how mental software can run on non-biological hardware is to think of mental states not in terms of physical implementation, but in terms of *functions*. Consider for example that one of the functions of the pancreas is to produce insulin which maintains the balance of sugar and salt in the body. It's easy to see that something else could perform this function, say a mechanical or silicon pancreas. Or consider an hourglass or an atomic clock. The function of both is to keep time, yet they do this quite differently.

Analogously, if mental states are identified by their functional role, then they too could be realized on other substrates, as long as the system performs the appropriate functions. In fact, once you have jettisoned the idea that your mind is a ghostly soul or a mysterious, non-physical substance, it's easy to see that your mind program could run on something besides a brain. It's certainly easy to imagine self-conscious computers or intelligent aliens whose minds run on something other than biological brains. Of course there's no way for us to know what it would be like to exist without a brain and body, but there's no convincing reason to think one couldn't have subjective experiences without physicality.

Perhaps our experiences would be even richer without a brain and body.

Would Immortality Be Boring?

We have so far ignored philosophical questions about what we would do in a simulated reality for an indefinitely long time. This is the question recently raised by the prominent Princeton neuroscientist Michael Graziano. He argues that the question isn't whether we will be able to upload our brains into a computer—he says we will—but what will we do with all that time?

I suppose that some may get bored with eternity and prefer annihilation. Some would get bored with the heaven they often say they desire. Some are bored now. So who wants to extend their consciousness so that they can love better and know more? Who wants to live long enough to have experiences that surpass our current ones in unimaginable ways? The answer is … many of us do. Many of us aren't bored so easily. And if we get bored we can always delete the program.

Many also worry about whether their uploaded mind is a just a copy of their consciousness, and not the real thing. But this distinction is trivial. When uploading becomes available most won't worry that they are just copying their consciousness. Whether they can upload into a genetically engineered body, a robotic body or to a virtual reality, most will gladly do so rather than die. After all, we are changing every moment and few worry that we are only a copy of ourselves from ten years ago. We wake up every day as little more than a copy of what we were yesterday, and few fret about that.

The situation does differ depending on whether or not the original survives. If the original "you" survives after being copied, then there would be as many "yous" as there are perfect copies. Yet these copies would immediately become different from each other as they proceed into the future. So copying yourself just creates many different people. Of course there is no good reason to make multiple copies of yourself.

If the uploading process destroys the original "you," then you have transferred your consciousness into as many bodies you choose to transfer it into, although again there is no imperative to copy or transfer yourself into multiple bodies. But the main point is that *there is no important distinction between being copied or transferred.* If you want to preserve your consciousness and have no other options, such metaphysical concerns will be irrelevant. Note also that this problem arises for religious believers who die and hope to wake up in heaven. Is the you that wakes up in heaven just a copy, or have you been transferred there? Again you probably don't worry about this—you just want to wake up!

Now suppose you are facing death with a decrepit body. A new technology promises to upload your memories, experiences, and all your other psychological characteristics to a robotic body, or a virtual reality. Suppose further that the technology has been well-tested and many friends tell you how great it's to exist in robotic bodies or virtual realities. Should you follow them? You may decide you don't trust the technology, or you may decide to die and hope that God or Allah will save you. But if you opt for the high-tech solution, philosophical concerns about whether this new you is a copy or a transfer will not stop you from uploading. Not if you want to live forever.

Can "We" Really Live in the Future?

However, maybe this is all wrong. Maybe *we* can't exist in the future. To see this, suppose that we cryogenically preserve ourselves. Even if our descendants revive us there is a chance that our minds will be too primitive to be properly rebooted. Future technologies may be incompatible with our archaic mind files. It would be as if we found an old floppy disk or early telephone, but no longer had the means to run them.

Alternatively our descendants might reboot our mind files, but find that our restored minds can't deal with their radically different future. In response our offspring might download their knowledge into our minds, so as to better prepare us for their new world, but find our memory capacity and processing speed insufficient to deal with the procedure. It might kill us to assimilate all their knowledge. Literally.

To handle all this new experience and information, our progeny could re-engineer our brains or create new ones for us. Either way it's hard to see how our personal identity survives. Once we have thirty-first century brains loaded with thirty-first century knowledge, we are thirty-first century beings. We would no longer be the twenty-first century persons we used to be.

To solve this problem our new brains could be engineered so that we have access to our old mind files—thereby preserving something of our personality. But even if we could occasionally enter our old minds, we might find these former experiences so primitive that we wouldn't want to remember them. Why remember being a twenty-first century hominoid when better experiences are available?

So our futures selves, operating on new brains, would stand in relation to our current selves as we now do to star stuff. We came from the stars, but we aren't stars. At some point our past lives would be so distant and unfamiliar, that our connection with them would be lost. So maybe *we* can't live in the future. We live, if we live at all, in this reality, in this time. And when that time ends, we do to.

And yet ... we do live in the future ... in a sense. When we imagine it, when we long for it, to some extent we are there. No, our little egos might not be there, that is a triviality best discarded. But as long as minds freely roam space and time we live on—within other minds. This may not be all we want, but it may be all we can get. No one expressed these sentiments as well as Bertrand Russell in his essay "How To Grow Old."

> The best way to overcome it [the fear of death]—so at least it seems to me—is to make your interests gradually wider and more impersonal, until bit by bit the walls of the ego recede, and your life becomes increasingly merged in the universal life. An individual human existence should be like a river: small at first, narrowly contained within its banks, and rushing passionately past rocks and over waterfalls. Gradually the river grows wider, the banks recede, the waters flow more quietly, and in the end, without any visible break, they become merged in the sea, and painlessly lose their individual being. The man who, in old age, can see his life in this way, will not suffer from the fear of death, since the things he cares for will continue. And if, with the decay of vitality, weariness increases, the thought of rest will not be unwelcome. I should wish to die while still at work, knowing that others will carry on what I can no longer do and content in the thought that what was possible has been done.

So we can make peace with death by accepting this compromised sense of immortality, but if we don't have to die then worries about accepting death evaporate. Russell's advice becomes irrelevant. Yes, worries about how *we* can live on in the future are still with us, but this is always true. The ten or twenty year old me doesn't exist now either. But as long as there is continuity between my

human self and my transhuman and post-human self, then that is
enough to say we survive in the ordinary sense. For what else
could it mean to survive?

The Overpopulation Objection

Many worry that radical life extension or the elimination of death
will lead to overpopulation and ecological destruction. In other
words, while it may be best for individuals to live forever, it might
be collectively disastrous. Readers may recognize this situation as
an instance of the "tragedy of the commons." Acting in their
apparent self-interest, individuals destroy a common good. It may
be convenient for individuals to pollute the air, earth, and water,
but eventually this is catastrophic for all. However, I don't believe
that overpopulation and its attendant problems should give anti-
aging research pause. Here are some reasons why.

If we have conquered death, then we may already be post-
humans living after the singularity. Such beings may not want to
propagate, since achieving a kind of immortality is a major
motivation for having children. Such beings may be independent of
the physical environment too—their bodies may be impervious to
environmental stressors, or they may not have bodies at all. In such
cases concerns about overpopulation would be irrelevant. I am not
saying that they *will* be irrelevant; I'm saying that the tragedy of
150,000 people dying every single day—100,000 of them from
age-related causes—is a huge price to pay for speculative
hypotheses about the future. We shouldn't assume that our
concerns as biological beings today will be relevant in the future.

Of course, I don't know how the future will unfold. But
preserving the minds that now exist may be a better survival
strategy than educating new ones. In the future we will probably
need educated and mature minds—their invaluable knowledge and

wisdom. So I argue that we should try to eliminate death, dealing with overpopulation—assuming we even have to—when the time comes. My suggestions may be considered reckless, but remember there is no risk-free way to proceed. Whatever we do, or don't do, has risks. If we cease developing technology we will not be able to prevent the inevitable asteroid strike that will decimate our planet; if we continue to die young we may not develop the intelligence necessary to design better technology. Given these considerations, we shouldn't let hypotheticals about the future deter our research into defeating death.

Note too that this objection to life-extending research could have been leveled at work on the germ theory of disease, or other life-extending research and technology in the past. Don't cure diseases because that will lead to overpopulation! Don't treat sick children because they might survive and have more children! I think most of us are glad we have a germ theory of disease, and happy that we treat sick children. Our responsibility is to help people live long, healthy lives, not worry that by doing so other negative consequence might ensue. We are glad that some of our ancestors decided that a twenty-five year life span was insufficient; we are happy that didn't worry that curing diseases and extending life might have negative consequences.

Most importantly, I believe it's immoral for us to reject anti-aging research and the technologies it will produce, thereby forcing future generations to die involuntarily. After anti-aging technologies are developed, the living should be free to choose to live longer, live forever, or even die young if they want to. But it would be immoral for us not to try to make death optional for them. *If we made decisions for them, we would be imposing our values on them; we would not be respecting their autonomy.* At the moment we tolerate a high death rate to compensate for a high birth rate, but our descendants may not share this value.

111

Chapter 5 – The Unimaginable Future

Death is like a bomb strapped to our chest. The bomb is with us from birth, and can detonate at any time. If it's in our power to remove that bomb for future generations, then we should. We shouldn't let hypothetical concerns about negative consequences deter our removing those explosives. I'd bet future generations will thank us for removing such bombs, and even if our descendants decide that a hundred years of consciousness is enough, they will probably be thankful that we gave them the option to live longer. I'd guess that higher forms of being and consciousness will want to preserve their being. They would want us to disarm the bomb.

The lovers of death don't want to disarm the bomb because its detonation, they believe, transports you to a better address—from earth to a heavenly paradise where your mind and body are eternally bathed in a salve of peace, love, and joy. That is often their justification for opposing the bomb's removal. The problem is this story is fictional. And we know that most people agree because when humans conquer death, when they learn to remove the bomb—they will. Those in the future who have the option to live forever will be *eternally* grateful that they have the real thing, instead of the empty promises we now pay for each Sunday in church. Consciousness has come a long way from its beginnings in a primordial soup, but there is so much farther to go. Let's put our childhood behind us, and make something of ourselves.

I will admit that if you believe that humans should accept their fate, that they were specially designed and created by the gods, that the divine plan includes evil and death, and that we shouldn't interfere with the god's plans, then you should condemn transhumanism. However, the chance that all these things are true is small. Moreover, the opposition to the advance of science and technology will not likely succeed. Most don't desire to go back to the middle ages, when believers prayed sincerely and then died miserably. Today some still consult faith healers, but the intelligent go to their physicians. Furthermore, everything about technology plays god, and letting nature takes its course means that half the people reading this article—had they not benefitted from modern medicine—would have died from childhood diseases.

Still, there are good reasons to be cautious about designing and using future technologies, as Bill Joy outlined more than a decade ago in his article, "Why The Future Doesn't Need Us." But I reject Joy's suggestion that we relinquish new technologies. Yes, we should be cautious about implementing new technologies, but we shouldn't discard them. Do we really want to turn the clock back a hundred years before computers and modern medicine? Do we really want to freeze technology at its current level? Look before we leap, certainly, but leap we must. If we do nothing, eventually we will die: asteroids will hit the planet, the climate will change irrevocably, bacteria will evolve uncontrollably, and in the far future the sun will burn out. Only advanced technologies give us a chance against such forces.

If we do nothing we will die; if we gain more knowledge and the power that accompanies it, we have a chance. With no risk-free way to proceed, we should be brave and bold, unafraid to guide our own destiny.

The Transhumanist Wager

A better way to understand the risks and rewards of transhumanism—to reiterate the view that we should use science and technology to overcome all human limitations—is to think in terms of a wager. The Transhumanist Wager, brainchild of noted transhumanist Zoltan Istvan, is such a device and it can be understood as follows. If you love and value your life, then you will want the option to live as long and as well as possible. How do you achieve this? There are two alternatives.

Alternative #1 – Don't use science and technology to try to defeat death, and hope there is an afterlife. But since you don't know there is an afterlife, doing nothing doesn't help your odds.

Alternative #2 - Use science and technology to try to defeat death since doing something you are increasing your odds of being immortal.

The choice is between bettering your odds or not, and good gamblers recommend the former. There are two basic obstacles that prevent individuals from taking the wager seriously. First, most people don't think immortality is technologically possible or, if they do, believe such technologies won't be around for centuries or millennia. Most are unaware that research on life-extending and death-eliminating technologies is progressing rapidly. Some researchers think we are only decades from extending life significantly, if not defeating death altogether.

Second, even if convinced that we can overcome death, many feel we shouldn't. I am always amazed at how many people—when confronted for the first time with the idea that technology may give them the option of living longer, happier, and healthier lives—claim to prefer death. Perhaps their current lives are just too unfulfilling to want more. Or perhaps the paradigm shift required is too great, guided as they are by superstition, ancient religion, distorted views of what's natural, or a general love of stasis and disdain for change—even if it means condemning their consciousness to oblivion!

In order to better clarify the transhumanist wager let's compare it to two other wagers—Pascal's Wager and the Cryonics Wager.

Pascal's Wager advances a pragmatic argument for the existence of the Christian God. Here it is in matrix form:

Choice of Belief	God Exists	God Doesn't Exist
I Do Believe In God	Infinitely Good!	About Even
I Don't Believe In God	Infinitely Bad!	About Even

It's simple. Bet that God exists, believe in God, and you either win big (heaven) or lose nothing (except perhaps a little time and money in church). Bet that god doesn't exist, bet that you don't believe in God, and you either lose big (hell) or win nothing (except perhaps saving a bit of time and money in church.) The expected outcome of betting that god exists is infinitely greater than betting the reverse. Thus the wise bet on that God exists.

The main reason this argument fails is that it assumes there is only a single God who rewards and punishes. But we don't know reality is like this. You might bet on the existence of the Christian God, but in the afterlife find that Allah or Zeus condemns you for your false beliefs. Or even if the Christian God exists, you can't be sure that your version of Christianity is correct. Perhaps only 1 of the approximately 41,000 sects of Christianity is true; the version you believe is incorrect; and you will be condemned for your false beliefs.

Or consider another scenario. You believe in the inerrancy of the Bible, go to church, do good deeds, and are awoken at the last judgment by the Christian God. You're feeling pretty good, until you hear a voice say: "I made you in my image by giving you reason. Yet you turned your back on this divine gift, believing in supernatural miracles and other affronts to reason. You believed in me without good reason or evidence. Be gone then! Only scientists and rationalists, those who used the precious gift of reason that I bestowed upon them, can enter my kingdom."

This scenario may not be true, but it's as plausible as typical religious explanations of what earns reward and punishment, and it is more just. But the main point is that Pascal's wager doesn't work because we don't know that there is a single god who rewards or punishes us based on whether we believe in him. We don't know if reality is like that.

Now consider the *cryonics wager*. What happens if I preserve my whole body or my brain? I might be awakened by post-human descendents as an immortal being in a heavenly world. I might be awakened by beings who torture me hellishly for all eternity. Or I might never wake up. Should I make this wager? Should I get a cryonics policy? I don't know. If I don't preserve myself cryonically, then I might die and go to heaven, hell, or experience nothingness. If I do preserve myself, as we have just seen, similar outcomes await me.

In this situation all I can do is assess the probabilities. Does having a cryonics policy, as opposed to dying and taking my chances, increase or decrease my chances of being revived in a good reality? We can't say for sure. But if the policy increases that chance, if you desire a blissful immortality, and if you can afford a policy, then you should get one.

Personally I believe that having a cryonics policy greatly increases your chance of being revived in a better reality than dying and taking your chances. I place more faith in my post-human descendants than in unseen supernatural beings. Still I can understand why others would make a different choice, and we should respect their autonomy to die and hope for the best. In the end we just can't say for certain what the best move is.

Now recall the transhumanist wager:

Do nothing (scientifically) about death -> the odds for immortality are unaffected.

Do something (scientifically) about death -> the odds for immortality improve.

Thus, doing something is better than doing nothing.

Unfortunately alternative #2 is problematic. You don't know that doing something to eliminate death increases your odds of being immortal. Perhaps there are gods who favor you doing nothing. Perhaps they think that doing something to defeat death displays hubris. I don't believe this myself, but it's possible. On the other hand, the gods may favor those who try to defeat death. Moreover, as was previously discussed, even if you do achieve immortality you can't be sure it will be desirable. On the other hand, technologically achieved immortality may be wonderful.

Again the problem, as was the case with the other wagers, is that we just don't know the nature of ultimate reality. No matter what we do, or don't do, we may reap infinite reward, its opposite, or fade into oblivion. We can never know, from an infinite number of possibilities, what the future has in store for us. We can never know with certainty how we should wager.

Still not knowing for certain where to place our bet doesn't mean that some bets aren't better than others. Consider again are the three wagers:

Pascal's wager - do nothing -> except have faith

Chapter 5 – The Unimaginable Future

Cryonics wager - do something -> use cryonics technology

Transhumanist wager - do something -> use other life-extending technology

The choice comes down to doing nothing—except hoping that you have the right religious beliefs to enter into a blissful immortality—or doing something—buying a cryonics policy and/or supporting scientific research to defeat death. So what should you do?

Perhaps the best way to illuminate the choice is to consider a previous choice human beings faced in their history. What should they have done about disease? Should they have prayed to the gods and have faith that the gods will cure them, or should they have used science and technology to find the cures themselves? In hindsight the answer is clear. Praying to the gods makes no difference, whereas using modern medicine has limited death and disease, and nearly doubled the human life-span in the last century. When medieval Europeans contracted the plague they prayed hard … and then died miserably. Other examples easily come to mind. What is the best way to predict weather, harness energy, capture sound, achieve flight, communicate over great distances, or fly to far off planets? In none of these cases is doing nothing and hoping for the best a good bet. All of the above were achieved through the use of science and technology.

These examples highlight another advantage to making the transhumanist wager—the incremental benefits that accrue alongside longer and better lives as we approach the holy grail of a blissful immortality. Such benefits provide assurance that we are on the right path, which should increase our confidence that we are making the correct wager. In fact, the benefits already bestowed upon us by science and technology confirm that it is the best path toward a better future. As these benefits accumulate and as we become aware of them, our existence will become increasingly indistinguishable from the most enchanting descriptions of any afterlife.

So we should throw off archaic superstitions and use our technology. Will we do this? I can say with confidence that when an effective pill that stops or reverses aging becomes available at your local pharmacy—it will be popular. Or if, as you approach death, you are offered the opportunity to have your intact consciousness transferred to your younger cloned body, a genetically engineered body, a robotic body, or into a virtual reality, most will use such technologies when they have been shown to be effective. By then almost everyone will prefer the real thing to a leap of faith. At that point there will be no need to make a transhumanist wager. The transhumanist will already have won the bet.

Let us turn now to perhaps the ultimate question of human existence—the question of the meaning of life.

Chapter 6 – The Meaning of Life

The Search for Meaning

Life is hard. It includes physical pain, mental anguish, poverty, hatred, war and death. Life's problems are so significant that humans try desperately to alleviate and avoid them. But mere words cannot convey the depth and intensity of the suffering in human life. Consider that persons are starving, imprisoned, tortured, and suffering unimaginably as you read this; that our emotional, moral, physical, and intellectual lives are limited by our genes and environments; that our creative potential is wasted because of unfulfilling or degrading work, unjust incarceration, unimaginable poverty, and limited time; and that our loved ones suffer and die—as do we. Contemplate the horrors of history, and lives so insufferable that death was often welcomed. What kind of life is this that nothingness is often preferable? There is, as Unamuno said, a "tragic sense of life." This idea haunts the intellectually honest and emotionally sensitive individual. Life sometimes seems not worth the trouble.

Of course the above does not describe all of human life or history. There is love, friendship, honor, knowledge, play, beauty, pleasure, creative work, and a thousand other things that make life, at least sometimes, worthwhile, and at other times pure bliss. There are parents caring for their children, people building homes, artists creating beauty, musicians making music, scientists accumulating knowledge, philosophers seeking meaning, and children playing games. There are trees, flowers, mountains and oceans; there is art, science, literature and music; there is Rembrandt, Darwin, Shakespeare, and Beethoven. Life sometimes seems too good for words.

Now assuming that we are lucky enough to be born without any of a thousand physical or mental maladies, or into bondage, famine or war, the first problems we confront are how to feed, clothe, and shelter ourselves. Initially we have no choice but to rely on others to meet our basic needs, but as we mature we are increasingly forced to fulfill these needs on our own. In fact most human effort, both historically and presently, expends itself attempting to meet these basic needs. The structure of a society may aid us in satisfying our needs to differing extents, but no society fulfills them completely, and many erect impediments that make living well nearly impossible. We often fail to meet our basic needs through no fault of our own.

But even if we are born healthy and into a relatively stable environment, even if all our basic needs are met, we still face difficulties. We seek health and vitality, friends and mates, pleasure and happiness. Our desires appear unlimited. And presuming that we fulfill these desires, we still face pressing philosophical concerns: What is real? What can we know? What should we do? What can we hope for? And, most importantly, what is the meaning of life in a world that contains so much suffering and death? This is the central philosophical question of human life. Fortune may shine upon us, but we ultimately suffer and perish. And if all our hopes, plans and loves ultimately vanish, then what does it all mean? This question is not just academic; it penetrates to the core of the human existence.

Given the gravity of our query everyone, if they are lucky enough to have the chance, should think deeply about questions of meaning. And they should be honest in their quest, never cheating like the youths that Kierkegaard described: "There are many people who reach their conclusions about life like schoolboys: they cheat their master by copying the answer out of a book without having worked the sum out for themselves." If we work out the answers for ourselves then perhaps we will find that Rainer Marie Rilke was right when he said: "Live your questions now, and perhaps even without knowing it, you will live along some distant day into your answers."

The Question and Possible Answers

Albert Camus opens his essay "The Myth of Sisyphus" with these haunting lines: "There is but one truly serious philosophical problem, and that is suicide. Judging whether life is or is not worth living amounts to answering the fundamental question of philosophy." Karl Jaspers wrote: "The question of the value and meaning of existence is unlike any other question: man does not seem to become really serious until he faces it." Victor Frankl said: "man's search for meaning is the primary motivation of his life" and "… concern about a meaning of life is the truest expression of the state of being human." And the late, contemporary philosopher Robert Solomon considered the question of life's meaning to be "the ultimate question of philosophy." While major philosophers in the Western tradition have had much to say about the goal or final end of a human life, most have not—until the twentieth century—specifically addressed the question of life's meaning, and many have avoided it altogether.

In the Western world this lack of concern with the question of the meaning of life was in large part due to the domination of the Christian worldview. During the long period from about the 5th through the 18th century, the question of life's meaning was not especially problematic, since the answer was obvious. That answer was, roughly, that the meaning of life was to know, love, and serve god in this life, and to be with him forever in heaven. According to this view all the suffering of the world would be redeemed in the afterlife so that the sorrows of the world could be seen to have been worth it in the end, when we are united with god. However, with the decline of the influence of this worldview in subsequent centuries, the question of the meaning of life became a more pressing one, as we see beginning with nineteenth century thinkers such as Nietzsche and Schopenhauer. In the twentieth century the question took on a new urgency and western philosophers have increasingly written on the subject. Thus, with the exception of Schopenhauer, our text will concentrate exclusively on twentieth and twenty-first century thinkers.

My own view is that the question of life's meaning is the most important philosophical question, and possibly the most important question of any kind. This is not to say that it should be the only thing one thinks about; or that noble things cannot be done or happy lives cannot be lived without thinking about it. In fact one can think too much about it and, in the worst cases, compulsive analysis may lead to or manifest mental illness. Socrates claimed that "the unexamined life is not worth living," but the over-examined life is certainly not worth living either. Life may simply be too short to spend too much of one's life thinking about life. (The Latin "primum vivere deinde philosophare," translates to "First live, later philosophize.") Many persons in all walks of life have lived good and happy lives without thinking deeply about meaning, or without answering the question even if they have thought much about it. In short, philosophers should not overestimate the importance of their ruminations.

Still, such an important question demands some reflection. Without a tentative answer to the question there seems to be no ultimate justification for any action, or even a reason to be at all. To put it somewhat differently: What is the point of living, if you don't know the point of living? Why do anything, if you don't know why you should do anything? You might answer that you live because you have a will to live or a self-preservation instinct; but that merely explains why you do go on, it does not justify why you should go on. Of course you can certainly remain alive without thinking about these questions, and circumstances force many people to spend their lives trying to survive, leaving little time for philosophical contemplation. But for those with sufficient leisure time, for those that have their basic needs met, do they not have some obligation to think about the meaning of their lives, and by extension the meaning of life in general? Might not such thinking improve their lives and benefit others? If so, then thinking about the question of meaning is certainly worthwhile.

Here is a list of the basic answers to the question of the meaning of life that have been proposed:

1) Nihilistic answers—life is meaningless;

   Affirmation—it is good that life is meaningless;
   Acceptance—it is bad that life is meaningless, but we accept this;
   Rejection—it is bad that life is meaningless, and we reject this;

2) Agnostic answers—we don't know if life is meaningful;

   Meaningless—the question is unintelligible;
   Unanswerable—the question is intelligible, but we don't know if we can answer it;

3) Positive answers—life is meaningful;

   Supernatural (theistic) answers—meaning from transcendent gods;

   Natural (non-theistic) answers—meaning discovered/created in the natural world:

   i. meaning is objective—found by individuals;
   ii. meaning is subjective— invented by individuals.

Religious Answers: Tolstoy, James, Hick

A straightforward and emotionally appealing response to the problem of life's meaning is that of the religions. Although they vary widely in terms of their beliefs, generally they attempt to solve the main problems of life—of evil, suffering, death and meaning—by appealing to a god or gods. Religions typically argue that suffering is meaningful or will be remedied, that our needs for justice will be satisfied, and that death will be overcome either in an afterlife, or by escaping the wheel of birth and rebirth, or by some other supernatural scenario.

We begin with a caveat. It is impossible to discuss adequately the wide variety of religious expressions and experiences in the space allotted me—there are about 38,000 denominations of Christianity alone in the world today.

No doubt other religions are varied as well. Differences between denominations are themselves so vast that it is hard to recognize them as the same religion. What does St. Augustine's rejection of biblical literalism or the subtle theology of St. Thomas Aquinas have in common with modern Biblical fundamentalism? How similar is Shankara's absolute non-dualistic Vedanta to the beliefs of a typical Hindu? The answer is, in both cases, not much. Moreover, if you also consider that individuals within denominations have different understandings of their faiths, one could plausibly claim that there are as many types of religious beliefs as there are religious believers! Such considerations make an exhaustive discussion of religious answers to the meaning of life impossible.

Other questions arise too. What is religion? Is Buddhism a religion? Is Christianity? Is science motivated by religious impulses? Is any search for truth ultimately religious in its nature? Soren Kierkegaard, probably the most important Christian theologian of the 19th century, did not think that calling yourself a Christian, attending church, or ascribing to dogmas made you a Christian. So what does make you a Christian, Muslim, or Hindu? The answer is that we really don't know. Given these considerations—that religion is varied, multifaceted, and hard to define—it is obvious that religions answer the question in multiple ways. Thus we'll look at a few religious answers to our question, those of Leo Tolstoy, William James, and John Hick.

Tolstoy: A Crisis of Meaning and a Leap of Faith

Leo Tolstoy (1828 –1910) was a Russian writer widely regarded as among the greatest of novelists. His masterpieces *War and Peace* and *Anna Karenina* represent some of the best realistic fiction ever penned. He also was known for his literal interpretation of the teachings of Jesus, particularly those of the Sermon on the Mount, and he later became a pacifist and Christian anarchist. His ideas of non-violent resistance influenced Mahatma Gandhi and Martin Luther King. Near the end of his life, he finally rejected his wealth and privilege and became a wandering ascetic, dying in a train station shortly thereafter. The following summary is from a short work entitled: "A Confession" written in 1882, and first published in 1884. Tolstoy was one of the first thinkers to pose the problem of life's meaning in a modern way.

Tolstoy says he wrote to make money, take care of his family, and to forget questions about the meaning of life. But later—when seized with questions about the meaning of life and death—he came to regard his literary work as a waste of time. Without an answer to questions of meaning, he was incapable of doing anything. Despite fame, fortune, and family, he wanted to kill himself; being born, he said, was a stupid trick that was played on him. "Sooner or later there would come diseases and death…all my affairs…would sooner or later be forgotten, and I myself would not exist. So why should I worry about all these things." Life was represented for Tolstoy by an Eastern parable where a man hangs onto a branch inside of a well, with a dragon at the bottom, a beast at the top, and the mice eating the branch to which he clings. There is no way out and the pleasures of life—honey on the branch—are ruined by our inevitable death. Everything leads to the truth: "And the truth is death." The recognition of death and the meaninglessness of life ruin the joy of life.

The sciences provide some knowledge but this type of knowledge does not give comfort, and the kind of knowledge which would give comfort—knowledge about the meaning of life—does not exist. One is left with the realization that all is incomprehensible. Tolstoy suggests that the feeling of meaninglessness comes more often to the learned than to the simple people. Thus he began to look to the working class for answers, individuals who both ask and answer the question of the meaning of life. He notes that they did not derive meaning from pleasure, since they had so little of it, and yet they thought suicide to be a great evil. It seemed then that the meaning of life was not found in any rational, intellectual knowledge but rather "in an irrational knowledge. This irrational knowledge was faith…" Tolstoy says he must choose between reason, from which it follows that there is no meaning, and faith, which entails rejecting reason. What follows is that if reason leads to the conclusion that nothing makes sense, then the rational is actually irrational. And if irrationality leads to meaning, then irrationality is really rational—presuming that one wants meaning rather than truth.

Tolstoy essentially argued that rational, scientific knowledge only gives you the facts; it only relates the finite to the finite, it does not relate a finite life to anything infinite. So that "no matter how irrational and monstrous the answers might be that faith gave, they had this advantage that they introduced into each answer the

127

relation of the finite to the infinite, without which there could be no answer." Only by accepting irrational things—the central tenets of Christianity—could one find an answer to the meaning of life. So one must have faith, but what is faith? For Tolstoy "faith was the knowledge of the meaning of human life...Faith is the power of life. If a man lives he believes in something." And he found this faith, not in the wealthy or the intellectuals, but in the poor and uneducated. The meaning given to the simple life by simple people … that was the meaning Tolstoy accepted. Meaning is found in a simple life and religious faith.

Summary – Questions about the meaning of life are crucial, but our rational science cannot answer these questions. Thus we must adopt a non-rational solution; we must accept the non-rational faith of the simple person. Ironically, this non-rational faith is rational, since it provides a way to live.

James: Life is Worth Living if We Have Faith

William James (1842 – 1910) was trained as a medical doctor, was one of the most important figures in the history of American philosophy, and was a pioneering psychologist. He is the brother of the novelist Henry James, and friend of numerous intellectuals including: Ralph Waldo Emerson, Charles Sanders Peirce, Bertrand Russell, Josiah Royce, John Dewey, Mark Twain, Henri Bergson and Sigmund Freud. He spent his entire academic career at Harvard. The following is a summary of an address James gave to the Harvard YMCA in 1895 entitled: "Is Life Worth Living?"

James began by noting that some answer this question with a temperamental optimism that denies the existence of evil—for example the poet Walt Whitman and philosopher Rousseau. For both of them to breathe, to walk, or to sleep is joy or felicity itself. According to James, the problem with this approach is that such moods are impermanent, and the personalities that experience them are not universal; if they were, the question of whether life is worth living would not arise. Instead most of us oscillate between joy and sadness, between ecstasy and despair, and therefore for most of us the thought that life is not worth living occasionally arises. Almost anyone in the midst of some merriment and suddenly confronted with death, disease, and suffering, would find that their unabated exuberance about life quickly dispelled.

Suicide is evidence that not all individuals are temperamentally optimistic, and many more experience despondency after philosophical reflection. If such reflection about the ultimate nature of things breeds despair, how can reflection combat that gloom? James provides a preview to his answer: "Let me say, immediately, that my final appeal is to nothing more recondite than religious faith." The reason for this is that pessimism results from a religious demand that has not been satisfied. The chief source of this pessimism is our reflective grasp of the contradiction between the facts of nature and our desire to believe there is something good behind those facts. For the credulous such reflective pessimism does not surface, but for more scientific minded there are only two possible solutions to the apparent discord: 1) forgo a religious or poetic reading of reality and accept the bare facts of nature; or 2) adopt new beliefs or discover new facts to reconcile a religious reading of reality with the hard facts of science.

But what new religious beliefs might hasten this reconciliation? James claims that the essence of religious supernaturalism is the view that the natural order is part of a larger reality which in turn gives significance to our mundane existence and explains the world's riddles. These are the kinds of belief that might aid us in our search for meaning. James now presents a preview of his conclusion: "that we have a right to believe the physical order to be only a partial order; that we have a right to supplement it by an unseen spiritual order which we assume on trust ..."

Chapter 6 – The Meaning of Life

To those who claim that his approach is mystical or unscientific, James responds that science and the scientifically minded should not be arrogant. Science gives us a glimpse of what is real, but its knowledge is miniscule compared to the vastness of our ignorance. Agnostics admit as much but will not use their ignorance to say anything positive about the unknown, counseling us to withhold assent in matters where the evidence is inconclusive. James accepts such a view in the abstract, but neutrality cannot be maintained practically. If I refrain from believing in the supernatural, I express my refrain by acting as if the supernatural is not real; by not acting as if religion were true, one effectively acts as if it were not true. But science has no authority to deny the existence of an invisible world that gives us what the visible world does not. Science can only say what is, it cannot speak of what is not; and the agnostic prescription to proportion assent to evidence is merely a matter of taste.

The benefits of believing in an unseen spiritual world are practical and if we remove this comfort from human beings, suicidal despair may result. As for the claim that such belief is just wishful thinking, James reminds us how little we know of reality relative to omniscience. While such belief is based on the possibility of something rather than its confirmed reality, human lives and actions are always undertaken with uncertainty. If the only way off a mountain is to leap, then you must trust yourself and leap—if you hesitate too long the outcome is certain death. Although we cannot be sure of much, it is best to believe in the practical, in that which helps us live.

For James the issue of whether life is worth living is similar. You can accept a pessimistic view of life and even commit suicide— you can make something true for yourself by believing it. But suppose instead you cling to the view that there is something good beyond this world? Suppose further that your subjectivity will not

130

yield to gloom, that you find joy in life. Have you not then made life worth living? Yes, we can make our lives worth living with our optimism. So it is our faith in an unseen world, in a religious or spiritual world, that grounds our belief in this world's worthiness. Courage means risking one's life on mere possibility, and the faithful believe in that possibility. James concludes with the following exhortation:

> These, then, are my last words to you: Be not afraid of life. Believe that life is worth living, and your belief will help create the fact. The 'scientific proof' that you are right may not be clear before the day of judgment ... is reached. But the faithful fighters of this hour, or the beings that then and there will represent them, may then turn to the faint-hearted, who here decline to go on, with words like those with which Henry IV greeted the tardy Crillon after a great victory had been gained: "Hang yourself, brave Crillon! We fought at Arques, and you were not there."

Summary – We need to be optimistic and have faith in an unseen spiritual world for life to be meaningful.

Hick: Religion and Cosmic Optimism

John Hick (1922 - 2012) was a world-renowned authority and an advocate of religious pluralism. He is often described as the most significant philosopher of religion in the 20th century. He has taught at Cambridge, Birmingham, Princeton, Cornell, and Claremont Graduate School, and is the author of more than twenty five books.

His article "The Religious Meaning of Life" (2000) claims that religious meaning concerns itself with the question of the nature of the universe and our part in it, as well as whether the universe is ultimately hostile, benign, or indifferent to our concerns. His hypothesis is that the great world religions are characterized by cosmic optimism. "That is to say, the meaning of life is such that we can have an ultimate trust and confidence, even in life's darkest moments of suffering and sorrow."

This cosmic optimism means that our current state can be replaced by a better one and in the limitless good of nirvana, for example, meaning is found. Similar claims can be made for other great religions. The Christian gospels present the good news (the notion of eternal punishment undermines cosmic optimism but is not a biblical doctrine according to Hick), Judaism's optimism derives from the special relationship between god and his people, Islam affirms that the universe is benign and our lives will be fulfilled in paradise, and Hinduism teaches that we move toward liberation. Cosmic optimism provides the means by which various religions answer the question of life's meaning. Hick concludes:

> the meaning for us of our human life depends upon what we believe to be the nature of the universe in which we find ourselves. The great world religions teach that the process of the universe is good from our human point of view because its ultimate principle...or its governor ... is benign...This is basically a very simple and indeed ...obvious suggestion—though not necessarily any the worse for that.

Summary – The world's religions advocate a cosmic optimism which is characterized by the belief that the universe is benign and thusly meaningful.

Agnosticism: Ayer, Nozick, Wittgenstein

Agnosticism is the idea that the truth or falsity of some claim is unknown or unknowable; it also denotes a basic skepticism toward answering certain questions. Typically agnosticism applies to religious belief, but in our case the idea applies to the meaning of life. The authors we call agnostic believe either that the question of the meaning of life is meaningless or that the answer, if one exists, is unknowable. To better understand agnosticism regarding the question of life's meaning let's look at three philosophers who espoused this view. They are among the most famous philosophers of the twentieth-century—A.J. Ayer, Robert Nozick, and Ludwig Wittgenstein.

Ayer: A Meaningless Question and Subjective Values

A.J. Ayer (1910 – 1989) was the Grote Professor of the Philosophy of Mind and Logic at University College London from 1946 until 1959, when he became Wykeham Professor of Logic at the University of Oxford. He is one of the most important philosophers of the twentieth-century. Ayer is perhaps best known for advocating the verification principle, the idea that statements and questions are meaningful only if we can determine whether they are true by analytic or empirical methods.

In his 1947 article "The Claims of Philosophy," Ayer asks: does our existence have a purpose? According to Ayer to have a purpose means to intend, in some situation "to bring about some further situation which ... he [she] conceives desirable." (For example, I have a purpose if I intend to go to law school because that leads to becoming a lawyer which is something I consider desirable.) Thus events have or lack meaning to the extent they bring about, or do not bring about, the end that is desired. But how does "life in general" have meaning or purpose?

The above suggests that overall meaning would be found in the end to which all events are tending. Ayer objects that: 1) there is no reason to think that there is an end toward which all things are tending; and 2) even if there were such an end it would do us no good in our quest for meaning because the end would only explain existence (it is heading toward some end) not justify existence (it should move toward that end). Furthermore, the end would not have been one we had chosen; to us this end is arbitrary, that is, it is without reason or justification. So from our point of view, it does not matter whether we receive a mechanical explanation (the end is universal destruction) or a teleological explanation (the end is union with a god). Either way we merely explain how things are but we do not justify why things are—and that is what we want to know when we ask the meaning of life question. We want to know if there is an answer to this ultimate why question.

Now one might answer that the end toward which all is tending is the purpose of a superior being and that our purpose or meaning is to be a part of the superior being's purpose. Ayer objects that: 1) there is no reason to think that superior beings exist; and 2) even if there were superior beings it would do us no good in our quest for meaning because their purposes would not be our purposes. Moreover, even if superior beings had purposes for us, how could we know them? Some might claim this has been mysteriously revealed to them but how can they know this revelation is legitimate? Furthermore, allowing that superior beings have a plan for us and we can know it, this is still not enough. For either the plan is absolute—everything that happens is part of the plan—or it is not. If it is absolute then nothing we can do will change the outcome, and there is no point in deciding to be part of the plan because by necessity we will fulfill our role in bringing about the superior being's end. But if the plan is not absolute and the outcome may be changed by our choices, then we have to judge whether to be part of the plan. "But that means that the significance of our behavior depends finally upon our own judgments of value; and the concurrence of a deity then becomes superfluous."

Thus invoking a deity does not explain the why of things; it merely pushes the why question to another level. In short even if there are deities and our purpose is to be found in the purposes they have for us, that still does not answer questions such as: why do they have these purposes for us? Why should we choose to act in accord with their plans? And regarding the answers to these questions we can simply ask why again. No matter what level of explanation we proceed to, we have merely explained how things are but not why they are. So the ultimate why question—why does anything at all exist—is unanswerable. "For to ask this is to assume that there can be a reason for our living as we do which is somehow more profound than any mere explanation of the facts..." So it is not that life has no meaning. Rather it is the case that it is logically impossible to answer the question—since any answer to why always leads to another why. This leads Ayer to conclude that the question is not factually significant.

However, there is a sense in which life can have meaning; it can have the meaning or purpose we choose to give it by the ends which we choose to pursue. And since most persons pursue many different ends over the course of their lives there does not appear to be any one thing that is the meaning of life. Still, many search for the best end or purpose to pursue, hence the question of meaning is closely related to, or even collapses into, the question: how should we live? But that issue cannot be resolved objectively since questions of value are subjective. In the end each individual must choose for themselves what to value; they must choose what purposes or ends to serve; they must create meaning for themselves.

Summary of Ayer - There is no reason to think there is a purpose or final end for all life and even if there were one, say it was to fulfill a god's purpose, that would be irrelevant since that purpose would not be ours. Regarding such a plan either we cannot help but

135

be part of it—in which case it does not matter what we do—or we must choose whether to be part of it—which means meaning is found in our own choices and values. Moreover, all this leads us to ask what is the purpose or meaning of the gods' plans; but any answer to that question simply begets further why questions indefinitely. Thus it is logically impossible to answer the ultimate why question. In the end, the question of the meaning of life dissolves into or reduces to the question of how we should live.

Nozick: How Can Anything Glow Meaning?

Robert Nozick (1938 – 2002) was an American political philosopher and professor at Harvard University. He is best known for his book *Anarchy, State, and Utopia* (1974), a libertarian answer to John Rawls's *A Theory of Justice* (1971). In chapter six of his 1981 book, *Philosophical Explanations*, Nozick addresses the question of the meaning of life.

"The question of what meaning our life has, or can have, is of utmost significance to us." Yet we try to hide our concern about the question by making jokes about it. So what do we seek when asking this question? Basically we want to know how to live in order to achieve meaning. We may choose to continue our present life in the suburbs, change our lives completely by moving to a cave and meditating daily, or opt for a number of other possibilities. But how is one to know which life is really most meaningful from an infinite number of choices? "Could any formula answer the question satisfactorily?"

A formula might be the meaning of life: seek union with a god, be productive, search for meaning, find love, etc. Nozick finds none of the proposed formulas satisfactory. Do we then seek some secret verbal formula or doctrine? Suppose there were a secret formula possessed by the sages. Would they give it to you? Would you be able to understand it? Maybe the sage will give you a ridiculous answer just to get you thinking. Perhaps it is not words at all but the physical presence of the sage that will convey the truth the questioner seeks. By being in their presence over time you may come to understand the meaning of life even if meaning transcends verbal formulas. Nozick doubts all of this.

Now what about the idea that the meaning of life is connected with a god's will, design or plan? In this case the meaning of life is to fulfill the role the gods have fashioned for us. If we were designed and created for a purpose connected to a plan then that is what we are for—our purpose would be to fulfill that plan. Different theological variants of your purpose might be to merge with the gods or enjoy eternal bliss in their presence.

Now let us suppose there are gods, that they have created us for a purpose, and that we can know that purpose. The question is, even knowing that all of the above is true, how does this provide meaning for our lives? Suppose for example that our role in the divine plan was trivial. Say it was to provide CO_2 for plants. Would that be enough? No, you probably think your role needs to be more important than that. Not just any role will do, especially not a trivial one.

Moreover, we want our role to "be positive, perhaps even exalted." We don't want our role to be providing food for space aliens, however good we taste to them. Instead we want our role to focus on important aspects of ourselves like our intelligence or morality. But even supposing that we were to aid the space aliens by exercising our intelligence and morality that would not give us meaning if there was no point to us helping them. We want there to be a point to the whole thing.

Nozick argues that there are two ways we could be part of or fulfill a god's plan: 1) by acting in a certain way; or 2) by acting in any way whatsoever. Concerning the first we may wonder why we should fulfill the plan, and about both we may wonder how being a part of the plan gives our lives meaning. It may be good from the god's perspective that we carry out their plans, but how does that show it is good for us, since we might be sacrificed for some greater good? And even if it were good for us to fulfill their plan how does that provide us meaning? We might think it good to say help our neighbors and still doubt that life has meaning. So again how do the god's purposes give our lives meaning? Merely playing a role or fulfilling a purpose in someone else's plan does not give your life meaning. If that were the case your parent's plan for you would be enough to give your life meaning. So in addition to having a purpose, the purpose must be meaningful. And how do a god's purposes guarantee meaning? Nozick does not see how they could.

Accordingly you can: 1) accept meaninglessness, and either go on with your life or end it; 2) discover meaning; or 3) create meaning. Nozick claims 1 has limited appeal, 2 is impossible, so we are left with 3. You can create meaning by fitting into some larger purpose but, if you do not think there is any such purpose, you can seek meaning in some creative activity that you find intrinsically valuable. Engaged in such creative work, worries about meaninglessness might evaporate. But soon concerns about meaning return, when you wonder whether your creative activity has purpose. Might even the exercise of my powers be ultimately pointless? (This sends a chill through someone writing a book.)

Now suppose my creation, for example a book on the meaning of life, fits into my larger plan, to share my discoveries with others or leave something to my children. Does this give my creative activity meaning? Nozick doubts this solution will work since the argument is circular. That is, my creative activity is given meaning by my larger plan which in turn has meaning because of my creative activity. Moreover, what is the point of the larger plan? It was only chosen to give a meaning to life, but that does not show us what the plan is or what it should be.

This all brings Nozick back to the question of how our meaning connects to a god's purposes. If it is important that our lives have meaning, then maybe the god's lives are made meaningful by providing our lives with meaning, and our lives made meaningful by fitting into the god's plans. But if we and the gods can find meaning together, then why can't two people find it similarly? If they can then we do not need gods for meaning. Nor does it help to say that knowing the god's plan will give life meaning. First of all many religions say it impossible to know a god's plans, and even if we did know the plan this still does not show that the plan is meaningful. Just because a god created the world does not mean the purpose for creating it was meaningful, anymore than animals created by scientists in the future would necessarily have meaningful lives. It might be that directly experiencing a god would resolve all doubts about meaning. But still how can a god ground meaning? How can we encounter meaning? How can all questions about meaning end? "How, in the world (or out of it) can there be something whose nature contains meaning, something which just glows meaning?"

Summary – A god's purposes do not guarantee meaning for you. Rather than accept meaninglessness or try to discover meaning, Nozick counsels us to create meaning. Still, this might not be enough to really give our lives meaning. In the end, does anything emanate meaning? Can anything glow meaning? Nozick is skeptical.

Chapter 6 – The Meaning of Life

Wittgenstein: Meaningless Question or Ineffable Answer?

Ludwig Josef Johann Wittgenstein (1889 –1951) was an Austrian philosopher who held the professorship in philosophy at the University of Cambridge from 1939 until 1947. He first went to Cambridge in 1911 to study with Bertrand Russell who described him as: "the most perfect example I have known of genius as traditionally conceived, passionate, profound, intense, and dominating." Wittgenstein inspired two of the century's primary philosophical movements, logical positivism and ordinary language philosophy, and is generally regarded as one of most important philosophers of the twentieth century.

Given his stature as a 20th century giant of philosophy, we would be remiss if we did not mention Wittgenstein's doubt regarding the sensibility of our question, with the caveat that his positions are notoriously difficult to pin down and that we cannot, in this short space, due justice to the depth of his thought. To get the briefest handle on his thought on the question of the meaning of life, we will ruminate briefly upon the haunting lines that conclude his *Tractatus Logico-Philosophicus*:

> For an answer which cannot be expressed the question too cannot be expressed. The riddle does not exist. If a question can be put at all, then it can also be answered. Skepticism is not irrefutable, but palpably senseless, if it would doubt where a question cannot be asked. For doubt can only exist where there is a question; a question only where there is an answer, and this only where something can be said. We feel that even if all possible scientific questions be answered, the problems of life have still not been touched at all. Of course there is then no question left, and just this is the answer. The solution of the problem of life is seen in the vanishing of this problem.(Is not this the reason why men

to whom after long doubting the sense of life became clear, could not then say wherein this sense consisted?) There is indeed the inexpressible. This shows itself; it is the mystical ...Whereof one cannot speak, thereof one must be silent.

One problem with these famous lines is that they are open to at least two different interpretations. On one interpretation the question of the meaning of life lacks meaning; hence there is no answer to a meaningless question. Worries about the question end when we forget it and start living, but this is not the same as learning an answer—there is no answer to a meaningless question. On the other interpretation there is an answer to the question but we cannot say what it is—the answer is ineffable. If we take the question in the first way, then we no longer have to worry about it since there is nothing to know. If we take the question the second way, then we are somewhat comforted by the existence of a truth which cannot be spoken.

The problem is that the two interpretations are in tension. How do we reconcile the claim that the question is meaningless with the claim that there is an ineffable answer? (One way to reconcile the two might be to say the inexpressible only reveals itself after the question has disappeared.) However we interpret Wittgenstein's enigmatic remarks, we can say this. If the question is senseless, then we waste our time trying to answer it. And if the answer is ineffable, then we waste our time trying to verbalize it. Either way there is nothing to say. Thus we probably ought to follow Wittgenstein's advice and simply "be silent."

Nihilism: Camus, Nagel, Critchley

Nihilism is the philosophical doctrine which denies the existence of one or more of those things thought to make life good such as knowledge, values, or meaning. A true nihilist does not believe that knowledge is possible, that anything is valuable, or that life has meaning. Nihilism also denotes a general mood of extreme despair or pessimism toward life in general.

The historical roots of contemporary nihilism are found in the ancient Greek thinkers such as Demosthenes, whose extreme skepticism concerning knowledge is connected with epistemological nihilism. But as historians of philosophy point out, many others including Ockham, Descartes, Fichte, and the German Romanticists contributed to the development of nihilism. The philosophy of Frederick Nietzsche is most often and most closely associated with nihilism, but it is not clear that Nietzsche was a nihilist. However, the philosopher who had the most influence upon Nietzsche, and who was definitely a nihilist, was Arthur Schopenhauer. We'll consider the nihilistic response to the question of life's meaning given by three giants of contemporary philosophy—Albert Camus, Thomas Nagel, and Joel Feinberg.

Camus: Revolt Against Nihilism

Albert Camus (1913 – 1960) was a French author, philosopher, and journalist who was awarded the Nobel Prize for Literature in 1957. He was a major philosopher of the 20th-century, with his most famous work being the novel *L'Étranger* (The Stranger). He is often cited along with Jean Paul Sartre as an existentialist, although Camus rejected the label. He died in a car accident in France.

In "The Myth of Sisyphus" (1955) Camus claims that the only important philosophical question is suicide—should we continue to live or not? That all the rest is secondary is obvious, says Camus, because no one dies for scientific or philosophical arguments; they usually abandon them when their life is at risk. Yet people do die because either they judge their lives meaningless or for reasons that give their lives meaning. This suggests that questions of meaning supersede all other scientific or philosophical questions. "I therefore conclude that the meaning of life is the most urgent of questions."

What interests Camus is what leads to suicide. He argues that "beginning to think is beginning to be undermined … the worm is in man's heart." The rejection of life emanates from deep within, and this is where its source must be sought. For Camus killing yourself is admitting that all of the habits and effort needed for living are not worth the trouble. As long as we accept reasons for life's meaning we continue, but as soon as we reject these reasons we become alienated—we become strangers from the world. This feeling of separation from the world Camus terms absurdity, and it is this feeling that leads to the contemplation of suicide. Still, most of us go on because we are attached to the world; we live out of habit.

But is suicide a solution to the absurdity of life? For those who come to believe in life's absurdity it is the only honest answer; one's conduct must follow from one's beliefs. Of course conduct does not always follow from belief. Individuals argue for suicide but continue to live; others profess that there is a meaning to life and choose suicide. Yet most persons are attached to this world by instinct, by a will to live that precedes philosophical reflection. Thus they elude questions of suicide and meaning by combining instinct with the hope that something gives life meaning. Yet the repetitiveness of life brings absurdity back to consciousness. In Camus' words: "Rising, streetcar, four hours in the office or factory, meal, four hours of work, meal, sleep, and Monday, Tuesday, Wednesday, Thursday, Friday, and Saturday…" So the question of suicide returns, forcing a person to confront and answer this essential question.

Chapter 6 – The Meaning of Life

And what of the death to which suicide leads? Of death we know nothing. "This heart within me I can feel, and I judge that it exists. This world I can touch, and I likewise judge that it exists. There ends all my knowledge, and the rest is construction." Furthermore, I cannot know myself intimately anymore than I can know death. "This very heart which is mine will forever remain indefinable to me. Between the certainty I have of my existence and the content I try to give to that assurance, the gap will never be filled. Forever I shall be a stranger to myself …" We know that we feel but our knowledge of ourselves ends there.

What makes life absurd then is our inability to have knowledge of ourselves and the world's meaning even though we desire such knowledge. "…what is absurd is the confrontation of this irrational and the wild longing for clarity whose call echoes in the human heart." The world could have meaning: "But I know that I do not know that meaning and that it is impossible for me just now to know it." This tension between our desire to know meaning and the impossibility of knowing it is the only important truth we can utter. Humans are tempted to leap into faith, but the honest ones will answer that they do not understand; they will learn "to live without appeal…" In large part this means recognizing that one does not have to live up to any higher purposes. In this sense we are free—living without appeal, living the best we can in the face of the absurd. Aware of our condition we exercise our freedom and revolt against the absurd—this is the best we can do.

Nowhere is the essence of the human condition made clearer than in the Myth of Sisyphus. Condemned by the gods to roll a rock to the top of a mountain whereupon its own weight would make it fall back down again, Sisyphus was condemned to this perpetually futile labor. His crimes had seemed slight, yet his preference for the natural world as compared to the darkness of the underworld was enough to incur the wrath of the gods: "His scorn of the gods, his hatred of death, and his passion for life won him that unspeakable penalty in which the whole being is exerted toward accomplishing nothing." For this he was condemned to everlasting torment. Camus describes the toil of Sisyphus and the accompanying despair he must have felt knowing his labor was futile.

Yet Camus sees something else in Sisyphus at that moment when he goes back down the mountain. Consciousness of his fate is the tragedy; yet consciousness also allows Sisyphus to scorn the gods which provides a small measure of satisfaction. Tragedy and happiness go together; this is the state of the world that we must accept. Fate decries that there is no purpose for our lives, but one can be the master of their response—that nothing can take away:

> This universe henceforth without a master seems to him neither sterile nor futile. Each atom of that stone, each mineral of that night-filled mountain, in itself forms a world. The struggle itself toward the heights is enough to fill a man's heart. One must imagine Sisyphus happy.

Summary – Life is essentially meaningless and absurd yet we can revolt against it and find some happiness for ourselves. Essentially Camus asks if there is a third alternative between acceptance of life's absurdity or its denial by accepting hopeful metaphysical propositions. Can we live without the hope that life is meaningful but without the despair that leads to suicide? If the contrast is posed this starkly it seems an alternative appears—we can proceed defiantly forward. We can live without faith, without hope, and without appeal. And we can be happy.

Nagel: Irony as a Response to Nihilism

Thomas Nagel (1937-) is a prominent American philosopher, author of numerous articles and books, and currently University

Chapter 6 – The Meaning of Life

Professor of Philosophy and Law at New York University where he has taught since 1980.

In "The Absurd," (1971) Nagel asks why people sometimes feel that life is absurd. For example people sometimes say that life is absurd because nothing we do now will matter in the distant future. But Nagel points out that the corollary of this is that nothing in the distant future matters now: "In particular, it does not matter now that in a million years nothing we do now will matter." Furthermore, even if what we do now does matter in a distant future, how does that prevent our present actions from being absurd? In other words, if our present actions are absurd then their mattering in the distant future can hardly give them meaning. For the mattering in the distant future to be important things must matter now. And if I claim definitely that what I do now will not matter in a million years then either: a) I claim to know something about the future that I do not know; or b) have simply assumed what I'm trying to prove—that what I do will not matter in the future. Thus the real question is whether things matter now—since no appeals to the distant future seem to help us answer that question.

Consider next the argument that our lives are absurd because we live in a tiny speck of a vast cosmos or in a tiny sliver of time. Nagel argues that neither of these concerns makes life absurd. This is evident because even if we were immortal or large enough to fill the universe, this would not change the fact that our lives are absurd, if they are absurd. Another argument appeals to death, to the fact that everything ends, and reasons to the conclusion that there is no final purpose for our actions. Nagel replies that many of the things we do in life do not need any further justification than their justification at the moment—when I am hungry I eat! Moreover, if the chain of justification must always lead to another justification, we would be caught in an infinite regress. In short

146

since justification must end somewhere if it is to be justification at all, it might as well end in life. Nagel concludes that the arguments just outlined fail but adds: "Yet I believe they attempt to express something that is difficult to state but fundamentally correct."

For Nagel the discrepancy between the importance we place on our lives from a subjective point of view and how gratuitous they appear objectively is the essence of the absurdity of our lives. "... the collision between the seriousness with which we take our lives and the perpetual possibility of regarding everything about which we are serious as arbitrary, or open to doubt." And, short of escaping life altogether, there is no way to reconcile the absurdity resulting from our pretensions and the nature of reality. This analysis rests on two points: 1) the extent to which we must take our lives seriously; and 2) the extent to which, from a certain point of view, our lives appear insignificant. The first point rests on the evidence of the planning, calculation, and concerns with which we invest in our lives.

> Think of how an ordinary individual sweats over his appearance, his health, his sex life, his emotional honesty, his social utility, his self-knowledge, the quality of his ties with family, colleagues, and friends, how well he does his job, whether he understands the world and what is going on in it. Leading a human life is full-time occupation to which everyone devotes decades of intense concern.

The second point rests on the reflections we all have about whether life is worth it. Usually after a period of reflection, we just stop thinking about it and proceed with our lives.

To avoid this absurdity we try to supply meaning to our lives through our role "in something larger than ourselves... in service to society, the state, the revolution, the progress of history, the advance of science, or religion and the glory of God." But this larger thing must itself be significant if our lives are to have meaning by participating in it; in other words, we can ask the same question about meaning of this larger purpose as we can of our lives—what do they mean? So when does this quest for justification end? According to Nagel it ends when we want it to. We can end the search in the experiences of our lives or in being part of a divine plan. But wherever we end the search, we end it arbitrarily. Once we have begun to wonder what the point of it all is; we can always ask of any proposed answer—and what is the point of that? "Once the fundamental doubt has begun, it cannot be laid to rest." In fact there is no imaginable world that could settle our doubts about its meaning.

Nagel further argues that reflection about our lives does not reveal that they are insignificant compared to what is really important, but that our lives are only significant by reference to themselves. So when we step back and reflect on our lives, we contrast the pretensions we have about the meaning of them with the larger perspective in which no standards of meaning can be discovered.

Nagel contrasts his position on the absurd with epistemological skepticism. Skepticism transcends the limitations of thoughts by recognizing the limitations of thought. But after we have stepped back from our beliefs and their supposed justifications we do not then contrast the way reality appears with an alternative reality. Skepticism implies that we do not know what reality is. Similarly when we step back from life we do not find what is really significant. We just continue to live taking life for granted in the same way we take appearances for granted. But something has changed. Although in the one case we continue to believe the external world exists and in the other case we continue to pursue our lives with seriousness, we are now filled with irony and resignation. "Unable to abandon the natural responses on which they depend, we take them back, like a spouse who has run off with someone else and then decided to return; but we regard them differently..." Still, we continue to put effort into our lives no matter what reason has to say about the irony of our seriousness.

Our ability to step back from our lives and view them from a cosmic perspective makes them seem all the more absurd. So what then are our options? 1) We could refuse to take this transcendental step back but that would be to acknowledge that there was such a perspective, the vision of which would always be with us. So we cannot do this consciously. 2) We could abandon the subjective viewpoint (our earthly lives) and identify with the objective viewpoint entirely, but this requires taking oneself so seriously as an individual that we may undermine the attempt to avoid the subjective. 3) We could also respond to our animalistic natures only and achieve a life that would not be meaningful, but at least less absurd than the lives of those who were conscious of the transcendental stance. But surely this approach would have psychological costs. "And that is the main condition of absurdity— the dragooning of an unconvinced transcendent consciousness into the service of an imminent, limited enterprise like a human life."

But we need not feel that the absurdity of our lives presents us with a problem to be solved, or that we ought to respond with Camus' defiance. Instead Nagel regards our recognition of absurdity as "a manifestation of our most advanced and interesting characteristics." It is possible only because thought transcends itself. And by recognizing our true situation we no longer have reason to resent or escape our fate. He thus counsels that we regard our lives as ironic. It is simply ironic that we take our lives so seriously when nothing is serious at all; this is the incongruity between what we expect and reality. Still, in the end, it does not matter that nothing matters from the objective view, so we should simply chuckle at the absurdity of our lives.

Summary – Life has no objective meaning and there is no reason to think we can give it any meaning at all. Still, we continue to live and should respond, not with defiance or despair, but with an ironic smile. Life is not as important and meaningful as we may have once suspected, but this is not a cause for sadness.

Critchley: Affirming Nihilism

Simon Critchley (1960 -) was born in England and received his PhD from the University of Essex in 1988. He is series moderator and contributor to "The Stone," a philosophy column in The New York Times. He is also currently chair and professor of philosophy at The New School for Social Research in New York City.

In his recent book, *Very Little Almost Nothing*, Critchley discusses various responses to nihilism. Those responses include those who: a) refuse to see the problem, like the religious fundamentalist who doesn't understand modernity; b) are indifferent to the problem, which they see as the concern of bourgeoisie intellectuals; c) passively accept nihilism, knowing that nothing they do matters; d) actively revolt against nihilism in the hope that they might mitigate the condition. He rejects all views that try to overcome nihilism—enterprises that find redemption in philosophy, religion, politics or art—in favor of a response that embraces or affirms nihilism. For Critchley the question of meaning is one of finding meaning in human finitude, since all answers to the contrary are empty. This leads him to the surprising idea that "the ultimate meaning of human finitude is that we cannot find meaningful fulfillment for the finite." But if one cannot find meaning in finitude, why not just passively accept nihilism?

Critchley replies that we should do more than merely accept
nihilism; we must affirm "meaninglessness as an achievement, as a
task or quest ... as the achievement of the ordinary or everyday
without the rose-tinted spectacles of any narrative of redemption."
In this way we don't evade the problem of nihilism but truly
confront it. As Critchley puts it:

> The world is all too easily stuffed with meaning and we
> risk suffocating under the combined weight of competing
> narratives of redemption—whether religious, socio-
> economic, scientific, technological, political, aesthetic or
> philosophical—and hence miss the problem of nihilism in
> our manic desire to overcome it.

For models of what he means Critchley turns to playwright
Samuel Beckett whose work gives us "a radical de-creation of
these salvific narratives, an approach to meaninglessness as the
achievement of the ordinary, a redemption from redemption."
Salvation narratives are empty talk which cause trouble; better to
be silent as Pascal suggested: "All man's miseries derive from not
being able to sit quietly in a room alone." What then is left after we
are saved from the fables of salvation? As his title suggests; very
little ... almost nothing. But all is not lost; we can know the
happiness derived from ordinary things.

Critchley finds a similar insight in what the poet Wallace Stevens
called "the plain sense of things." In Stevens' famous poem, "The
Emperor of Ice Cream," the setting is a funeral service. In one
room we find merriment and ice cream, in another a corpse. The
ice cream represents the appetites, the powerful desire for physical
things; the corpse represents death. The former is better than the
latter, and that this is all we can say about life and death. The
animal life is the best there is and better than death—the ordinary
is the most extraordinary.

For another example Critchley considers Thornton Wilder's famous play "Our Town" which exalts the living and dying of ordinary people, as well as the wonder of ordinary things. In the play young Emily Gibbs has died in childbirth and is in an afterlife, where she is granted her wish to go back to the world for a day. But when she goes back she cannot stand it; people on earth live unconscious of the beauty which surrounds them. As she leaves she says goodbye to all the ordinary things of the world: "to clocks ticking, to food and coffee, new ironed dresses and hot baths, and to sleeping and waking up." It is tragic that while living we miss the beauty of ordinary things. Emily is dismayed but we are enlightened—we ought to appreciate and affirm the extraordinary ordinary. Perhaps that is the best response to nihilism—to be edified by it, to find meaning in meaninglessness, to realize we can find happiness in spite of nihilism.

Summary – We should reject philosophies of meaning and affirm nihilism, enjoying nonetheless the pleasures that life offers.

Subjective Answers: Russell, Taylor, Hare

Assuming that none of our previous answers completely satisfies, we now consider the idea that meaning is not something you stumble upon, receive, or discover, but something you fashion, invent or create. This is probably the most prevalent view among contemporary philosophers. On this account life can still be meaningful even though there is no supernatural reality—but only if individuals give meaning to their lives in the natural world in which they live. Therefore subjectivists believe that meaning is relative to their desires, attitudes, interests, wants, preferences, etc., and there are no invariant standards of meaning. Something is meaningful to individuals to the extent that they find that thing meaningful, in other words, meaning is constituted by human minds and varies between persons. We'll consider three such answers from Bertrand Russell, Richard Taylor, and R.M. Hare.

Russell: Worshipping as a Free Man

Bertrand Arthur William Russell, 3rd Earl Russell, (1872 – 1970) was a British philosopher, logician, mathematician, historian, atheist, and social critic. He is considered, along with his protégé Ludwig Wittgenstein, one of the founders of analytic philosophy and is widely held to be one of the 20th century's most important logicians. He co-authored, with A. N. Whitehead, *Principia Mathematica*, an attempt to ground mathematics in logic. His writings were voluminous and covered a vast range of topics including politics, ethics, and religion. Russell was awarded the Nobel Prize in Literature in 1950 "in recognition of his varied and significant writings in which he champions humanitarian ideals and freedom of thought." Russell is thought by many to be the greatest philosopher of the 20th century.

Russell's view of the meaning of life is set forth most clearly in his 1903 essay: "A Free Man's Worship." It begins with an imaginary conversation about the history of creation between Mephistopheles, the devil, and Dr. Faustus, a man who sells his soul to the devil in return for power and wealth. In this account god had grown weary of the praise of the angels, and thought it might be more amusing to gain the praise of beings that suffered. Hence god created the world.

Russell describes the epic cosmic drama and how after eons of time the earth and human beings came to be. Humans, seeing how fleeting and painful life is before their inevitable death, vowed that there must be purpose outside of this world. And though following their instincts led to sin and the need for god's forgiveness, humans believed that god had a good plan leading to a harmonious ending for humankind. God, convinced of human gratitude for the suffering he had caused, destroyed man and all creation.

Russell argues that this not so uplifting story is consistent with the world-view of modern science. To elaborate he penned some of the most pessimistic and often quoted lines in the history of twentieth-century philosophy:

> That man is the product of causes which had no prevision of the end they were achieving; that his origin, his growth, his hopes and fears, his loves and his beliefs, are but the outcome of accidental collocations of atoms; that no fire, no heroism, no intensity of thought and feeling, can preserve an individual life beyond the grave; that all the labors of the ages, all the devotion, all the inspiration, all the noonday brightness of human genius, are destined to extinction in the vast death of the solar system, and that the whole temple of Man's achievement must inevitably be buried beneath the debris of a universe in ruins—all these things, if not quite beyond dispute, are yet so nearly certain, that no philosophy which rejects them can hope to stand. Only within the scaffolding of these truths, only on the firm foundation of unyielding despair, can the soul's habitation henceforth be safely built.

Still, despite the ultimate triumph of vast universal forces, humans are superior to this unconscious power in important ways—they are free and self-aware. This is the source of their value. But most humans do not recognize this, instead choosing to placate and appease the gods in hope of reprieve from everlasting torment. They refuse to believe that their gods do not deserve praise, worshiping them despite the pain the gods inflict. Ultimately they fear the power of the gods, but the god's power is not a reason for respect and worship. For respect to be justified, creation must really be good. But the reality of the world belies this claim; the world is not good and submitting to its blind power enslaves and ultimately kills us.

Instead let us courageously admit that the world is bad, but nevertheless love truth, goodness, beauty, and perfection, despite the fact that the universe will destroy such things. By rejecting this universal power and the death it brings, we find our true freedom. While our lives will be taken from us by the universe, our thoughts can be free in the face of this power. In this way we maintain our dignity.

However, we should not respond to the disparity between the facts of the world and its ideal form with indignation, for this binds our thoughts to the evil of the universe. Rather we ought to follow the Stoics, resigned to the fact that life does not give us all we want. By renouncing desires we achieve resignation, while the freedom of our thoughts can still create art, philosophy and beauty. But even these goods ought not to be desired too ardently or we will remain indignant; rather we must be resigned to accept that our free thoughts are all that life affords in a hostile universe. We must be resigned to the existence of evil, to the fact that death, pain, and suffering will take everything from us. The courageous bear their suffering nobly and without regret; their submission to power an expression of their wisdom.

Still, we need not be entirely passive in our renunciation either. We can actively create music, art, poetry and philosophy, thereby incorporating the ephemeral beauty of this world into our hearts, achieving the most that humans can achieve. Yet such achievements are difficult, for we must first encounter despair and dashed hopes so that we may be somewhat freed from the Fate that will engulf us all—freed by the wisdom, insight, joy, and tenderness that our encounter with darkness brings. As Russell puts it:

> When, without the bitterness of impotent rebellion, we have learnt both to resign ourselves to the outward rule of Fate and to recognize that the non-human world is unworthy of our worship, it becomes possible at last so to transform and refashion the unconscious universe, so to transmute it in the crucible of imagination, that a new image of shining gold replaces the old idol of clay.

In our minds we find the beauty that we create in the face of Fate and tragedy, and in this way we master the power of nature. Life is tragedy, but we need not give in; instead we can find the "beauty of tragedy" and embrace it. In death and pain there is sanctity, awe, and a feeling of the sublime. In the experience of such feelings we forget petty and trivial desires and, at least temporarily, transcend the loneliness and futility of being a human confronted with vast forces over which one has no control, and which do not care for us. To take the tragedy of life into one's heart, to feel it, but to respond with renunciation, wisdom, and charity, is the ultimate victory for man: "To abandon the struggle for private happiness, to expel all eagerness of temporary desire, to burn with passion for eternal things—this is emancipation, and this is the free man's worship." For Russell the contemplation of Fate and tragedy are the way we subdue them.

As for our fellow companions, all we can do is to ease their sorrow and sufferings and not add to the misery that Fate and death will bring. We can take pride that we did not add to their pain. Nonetheless the universe continues its inevitable march to universal death and humans are condemned to lose everything. All we can do is to cherish those brief moments when thought and love ennoble us, and reject the cowardly terror of less virtuous persons

who worship Fate. We must ignore the tyranny of reality that
continually undermines all of our hopes and dreams and
aspirations. As Russell so eloquently puts it:

> Brief and powerless in man's life; on him and all his race
> the slow, sure doom falls pitiless and dark. Blind to good
> and evil, reckless of destruction, omnipotent matter rolls on
> its relentless way; for man, condemned today to lose his
> dearest, tomorrow himself to pass through the gate of
> darkness, it remains only to cherish ... the lofty thoughts
> that ennoble his little day; disdaining the coward terrors of
> the slave of Fate, to worship at the shrine that his own
> hands have built; undismayed by the empire of chance, to
> preserve a mind free from the wanton tyranny that rules his
> outward life; proudly defiant of the irresistible forces that
> tolerate, for a moment, his knowledge and condemnation,
> to sustain alone, a weary but unyielding Atlas, the world
> that his own ideals have fashioned despite the trampling
> march of unconscious power.

Summary – There is no objective meaning in life. We should be
resigned to this, not believing otherwise just because it is
comforting, but strive nonetheless to actively create beauty, truth,
and perfection. In this way we achieve some freedom from the
eternal forces that will destroy us.

Richard Taylor: Engaging Our Wills

Richard Taylor (1919 – 2003) was an American philosopher
renowned for his controversial positions and contributions to
metaphysics. He advocated views as various as free love and
fatalism, and was also an internationally-known beekeeper. He
taught at Brown, Columbia and the University of Rochester, and

had visiting appointments at about a dozen other institutions. His best known book was Metaphysics (1963).

In the concluding chapter of his 1967 book, Good and Evil: A New Direction, Taylor suggests that we examine the notion of a meaningless existence so that we can contrast it with a meaningful one. He takes Camus' image of Sisyphus as archetypical of meaninglessness—pointless and eternal toil. Taylor notes that it is not the weight of the rock or the repetitiveness of the work that makes Sisyphus' task unbearable, it is rather its pointlessness. The same pointlessness may be captured by other stories—say by digging and then filling in a ditch forever. Crucial to all these stories is that nothing ever comes of such labor.

But now suppose that Sisyphus' work slowly built a great temple on his mountaintop: "then the aspect of meaninglessness would disappear." In this case his labors have a point, they have meaning. Taylor further argues that the subjective meaninglessness of Sisyphus' activity would be eliminated were the Gods to have placed within him "a compulsive impulse to roll stones." Implanted with such desires, the gods provide him the arena in which to fulfill them. While we may still view Sisyphus' toil meaningless from the outside, for externally the situation has not changed, we can now see that fulfilling this impulse would be satisfying to Sisyphus from the inside. For now he is doing exactly what he wants to do—forever.

Taylor now asks: is life endlessly pointless or not? To answer this question he considers the existence of non-human animals— endless cycle of eating and being eaten, fish swimming upstream only to die and have offspring repeat the process, birds flying halfway around the globe only to return and have others do likewise. He concludes that these lives are paradigms of meaninglessness. That humans are part of this vast machine is equally obvious. As opposed to non-human animals we may choose our goals, achieve them, and take pride in that achievement. But even if we achieve our goals, they are transitory and soon replaced by others. If we disengage ourselves from the prejudice we have toward our individuals concerns, we will see our lives to be like Sisyphus'. If we consider the toil of our lives we will find that we work to survive, and in turn pass this burden on to our children. The only difference between us and Sisyphus is that we leave it to our children to push the stone back up the hill.

And even were we to erect monuments to our activities, they too would turn slowly turn to dust. That is why, coming upon a decaying home, we are filled with melancholy:

> There was the hearth, where a family once talked, sang, and made plans; there were the rooms, here people loved, and babes were born to a rejoicing mother; there are the musty remains of a sofa, infested with bugs, once bought at a dear price to enhance an ever-growing comfort, beauty, and warmth. Every small piece of junk fills the mind with what once, not long ago, was utterly real, with children's voices, plans made, and enterprises embarked upon.

When we ask what it all was for, the only answer is that others will share the same fate, it will all be endlessly repeated. The myth of Sisyphus' then exemplifies our fate, and this recognition inclines humans to deny their fate—to invent religions and philosophies designed to provide comfort in the face of this onslaught.

But might human life still have meaning despite its apparent pointlessness? Consider again how Sisyphus' life might have meaning; again if he were to erect a temple through his labors. Notice not only that the temple would eventually turn to dust, but that upon completion of his project he would be faced with boredom. Whereas before his toil had been his curse, now its absence would be just as hellish. Sisyphus would now be "contemplating what he has already wrought and can no longer add anything to, and contemplating it for an eternity!"

Given this conclusion, that even erecting a temple would not give Sisyphus meaning, Taylor returns to his previous thought— suppose that Sisyphus was imbued with a desire to labor in precisely this way? In that case his life would have meaning because of his deep and abiding interest in what he was doing. Similarly, since we have such desires within us, we should not be bored with our lives if we are doing precisely what we have an inner compulsion to do: "This is the nearest we may hope to get to heaven…"

To support the idea that meaning is found in this engagement of our will in what we are doing, Taylor claims that if those from past civilizations or the past inhabitants of the home he previously described were to come back and see that what was once so important to them had turned to ruin, they would not be dismayed. Instead they would remember that their hearts were involved in those labors when they were engaged in them. "There is no more need of them [questions about life's meaning] now—the day was sufficient to itself, and so was the life." We must look at all life like this, its justification and meaning come from persons doing what "it is their will to pursue." This can be seen in a human from the moment of birth, in its will to live. For humans "the point of [their] living, is simply to be living…" Surely the castles that humans build will decay, but it would not be heavenly to escape from all this, that would be boredom: "What counts is that one should be able to begin a new task, a new castle, a new bubble. It counts only because it is there to be done and [one] has the will to do it."

Philosophers who look at the repetitiveness of our lives and fall into despair fail to realize that we may be endowed, from the inside, with the desire to do our work. Thus: "The meaning of life is from within us, it is not bestowed from without, and it far exceeds in both beauty and permanence any heaven of which men have ever dreamed or yearned for."

Summary – We give meaning to our lives by the active engagement our wills have in our projects.

R. M. Hare: Does Nothing Matters?

R.M. Hare (1919 – 2002) was an English moral philosopher who held the post of White's Professor of Moral Philosophy at the University of Oxford from 1966 until 1983 and then taught for a number of years at the University of Florida. He was one of the most important ethicists of the second half of the twentieth century.

Hare begins by telling the story of a happy 18 year old Swiss boy who stayed with Hare in his house at Oxford. After reading Camus' The Stranger the boy's personality changed, becoming withdrawn, sullen, and depressed. (The Stranger explores existential themes like death and meaning; its title character Meursault is emotionally alienated, detached, and innately passive.) The boy told Hare that after reading Camus he had become convinced that nothing matters. Hare found it extraordinary that the boy was so affected.

As a philosopher concerned with the meaning of terms, Hare asked the young boy what "matters" means, what does it mean to be matter or be important? The boy said that to say something matters "is to express concern about that something." But Hare wondered whose concern is important here? When we say the something matters, the question arises, "matters to whom?"

Usually it's the speakers concern that is expressed, but it could be someone else's concern. We often say things like "it matters to you" or "it doesn't matter to him." In these cases we refer not to our own concern, but to someone else's.

In Camus' novel the phrase "nothing matters" could express the view of the author, the main character, or the reader (the young boy.) It's not Camus' unconcern that is being expressed, since he was concerned enough to write the novel—writing the novel obviously mattered to Camus. It is clear in the novel that the main character does think that nothing matters—he doesn't care about hardly anything. Still, Hare thinks that even Meursault is concerned about some things.

Hare doesn't think it possible to be concerned about nothing at all, since we always choose to do one thing rather than another thereby revealing, however slightly, what matters to us. At the end of Camus' novel Meursault is so upset by the priest's offer of religion that he attacks him in a rage. This display of passion shows that something did matter to Meursault, otherwise he would have done nothing. Yet even supposing that nothing does matter to a fictional character: why should that matter to the Swiss boy? In fact the boy admitted that he cares about many things, which is to say that things do matter to him. Hare thinks the boy's problem was not to find things that matter, but to prioritize them. He needed to find out what he valued.

Hare claims that our values come from our own wants and the imitation of others. Maturing in large part is bringing these two desires together—the desire to have our own values and to be like others with the former taking priority. "In the end...to say that something matters for us, we must ourselves be concerned about it; other people's concern is not enough, however much in general we may want to be like them." Nonetheless we often develop our own values by imitating others. For instance we may pretend to like philosophy because we think our philosophy professor is cool, and then gradually we develop a taste for it. This process often works in the reverse; my parents want me to do x, so I do y. Eventually, through this process of conforming and non-conforming, we slowly develop our own values.

Hare concludes that things did matter to the young boy and he was just imitating Meursault by saying that nothing matters, just as he was imitating him by smoking. What the boy did not understand was that matter is a word that expresses concern; it is not an activity. Mattering is not something things do, like chattering. So the phrase "my wife chatters," is not like the phrase "my wife matters." The former refers to an activity; the latter expresses my concern for her. The problem comes when we confuse our concern with an activity. Then we start to look in the world for mattering and when we do not find things actively doing this mattering, we get depressed. We do not observe things mattering, things matter to us if we care about them. Mattering doesn't describe something things do, but something that happens to us when we care about things. To say nothing mattes is hypocritical; we all care about something. (Even if what we care about is that nothings seems to matter.)

As for his Swiss friend, Hare says he was no hypocrite; he was just confused about what the word matter meant. Hare also suggests that we are the kinds of beings who generally care about things, and those who sincerely care about almost nothing are just unusual. In the end we cannot get rid of values—we are creatures that value things. Of course when confronted with various values, so many different things about which to be concerned, it is easy to through up our hands and say that nothing matters. When confronted with this perplexity about what to be concerned about, about what to value, Hare says we might react in one of two ways.

163

First, we might reevaluate our values and concerns to see if they are really ours; or second, we might stop thinking about what is truly of concern altogether. Hare counsels that we follow the former course, as the latter alternative leads to stagnation: "We content ourselves with the appreciation of those things, like eating, which most people can appreciate without effort, and never learn to prize those things whose true value is apparent only to those who have fought hard to achieve it..."

Summary – We all generally care about some things, some things do matter to us. We don't find this mattering in the world; it is something we bestow upon things and persons. Hare suggests we find value (or meaning) in things which are really worthwhile.

Objective Answers: Rachels, Flanagan, Frankl

If one finds both the supernatural and subjective answers unsatisfying, then perhaps meaning is objective and found in the natural world. Objectivists believe that (at least some) meaning is independent of their desires, attitudes, interests, wants, and preferences; that there are invariant standards of meaning independent of human minds. Such meaning is not derived from a supernatural realm, but from objective elements in the natural world. However, this does not mean that value or meaning is exclusively objective, as the following thinkers recognize. Effort on the part of the subject is necessary to derive or discover the objective meaning in the world. We'll look at three contemporary philosophers who find objective meaning in the things of the natural world.

Rachels: Good Things Make Life Worth Living

James Rachels (1941- 2003) was a distinguished American moral philosopher and best-selling textbook author. He taught at the University of Richmond, New York University, the University of

Miami, Duke University, and the University of Alabama at Birmingham, where he spent the last twenty-six years of his career.

The final chapter of his book, Problems from Philosophy, explores the question of the meaning of life. Although Rachels admits the question of the meaning of life does come up when one is depressed, and hence can be a symptom of mental illness, it also arises when we are not depressed, and thus mental illness is not a prerequisite for asking the question. He agrees with Nagel that the questions typically results from recognizing the clash between the subjective or personal point of view—from which things matter— and the objective or impersonal view—from which they do not.

Regarding the relationship between happiness and meaning, Rachel notes that happiness is not well correlated with material wealth, but with personal control over one's life, good relationships with family and friends, and satisfying work. In Rachels' view happiness is not found by seeking it directly, but as a by-product of intrinsic values like autonomy, friendship, and satisfying work. Nonetheless, a happy life may still be meaningless because we die, and in times of reflection we may find our happiness undermined by the thought of our annihilation.

What attitude should we take toward our death? For those who believe they do not die, death is good because they will live forever in a hereafter. For them death "is like moving to a better address." But for those who believe that death is their final end, death may or may not be a good thing. What attitude should these people take toward death? Epicurus thought that death was the end but that we should not fear it, since we will be nothing when dead and nothingness cannot harm us. He thought that such an attitude would make us happier while alive. On the contrary, Rachels thinks that death is bad because it deprives us of, and puts an end to, all the good things in life. (This is a version of the deprivation argument discussed previously.)

Although death is bad it does necessarily make life meaningless, inasmuch as the value of something is different than how long it lasts. A thing can be valuable even if it is fleeting; or worthless even if it lasts a forever. So the fact that something ends does not, by itself, negate its value.

There is yet another reason that a happy life might be meaningless—and that reason is that the universe may be indifferent. The earth is but a speck in the inconceivable vastness of the universe, and a human lifetime but an instant of the immensity of time. The universe does not seem to care much for us. One way to avoid this problem is with a religious answer— claim that the universe and a god do cares for us. But how does this help, even if it is true? As we have seen, being a part of another's plan does not seem to help, nor does being a recipient of the god's love, or living forever. It is simply not clear how positing gods gives our lives meaning.

Rachels suggest that if we add the notion of commitment to the above, we can see how religion provides meaning to believer's lives. Believers voluntarily commit themselves to various religious values and hence get their meaning from those values. But while you can get meaning from religious values you can also get them from other things—from artistic, musical, or scholarly achievement for example. Still, the religious answer has a benefit that these other ways of finding meaning do not; it assumes that the universe is not indifferent. The drawback of the religious view is that it assumes the religious story is true. If it is not, then we are basing our lives on a lie.

But even if life does not have a meaning, particular lives can. We give our lives meaning by finding things worth living for. These differ between individuals somewhat, yet there are many things worth living for about which people generally agree—good personal relationships, accomplishments, knowledge, playful activities, aesthetic enjoyment, physical pleasure, and helping others. Could it nonetheless be that all of this amounts to nothing, that life is meaningless after all? From the objective, impartial view we may always be haunted by the suspicion that life is meaningless. The only answer is to explain why our list of good things is really good.

Such reasoning may not show that our lives are 'important to the universe,' but it will accomplish something similar. It will show that we have good, objective reasons to live in some ways rather than others. When we step outside our personal perspective and consider humanity from an impersonal standpoint, we still find that human beings are the kinds of creatures who can enjoy life best by devoting themselves to such things as family and friends, work, music, mountain climbing, and all the rest. It would be foolish, then, for creatures like us to live in any other way.

Summary - Happiness is not the same as meaning and is undermined by death. Death is bad unless religious stories are true, but they probably are not true. Thus, while there is probably no objective meaning to life, there are good things in life. We should pursue those good things that most people think worthwhile—love, friendship, knowledge, and all the rest.

Flanagan: Self-Expression Gives Life Meaning

Owen Flanagan (1949 -) is the James B. Duke Professor of Philosophy and Professor of Neurobiology at Duke University. He has done work in philosophy of mind, philosophy of psychology, philosophy of social science, ethics, moral psychology, as well as Buddhist and Hindu conceptions of the self.

Flanagan does not assume "that life is or can be worth living." Perhaps we are just biologically driven to live worthless lives. So he begins by asking: "Is life worth living?" And if it is then "…what sorts of things make it so?" He notes that reflecting on this question may be a waste of time, as life might be better for the non-reflective. Reflection may lead to despair, if one determines that life is worthless, or to joy, if one concluded to the contrary. The question of whether life is worth living and what makes it so is connected with another bewildering question: "Do we live our lives?" In one sense the answer is obvious—we spend time not dead—but Flanagan wants to know if we act freely or are merely controlled like puppets. So questions about the value of living involve issues about who we are and what kinds of things are true about us.

Flanagan argues that even happiness is not enough to guarantee that life is worthwhile, inasmuch as a life may contain much happiness and still be meaningless. Happiness is not sufficient for meaning, since one might derive happiness from evil things, and it may not be necessary either, since a meaningful life may be devoid of happiness. But even if happiness is a component of a worthwhile life, he argues that identity and self-expression are more crucial. "Wherever one looks, or so I claim, humans seek, and sometimes find worth in possessing an identity and expressing it." Identity and self-expression are necessary but not sufficient conditions for worthwhile living, since we need to clarify what forms of identity and expressions of it are valuable.

But what if there is no self to find meaning through self-expression? There are three standard arguments supporting the idea that we are not selves. First, maybe I am just a location where things happen from a universal perspective. Second, I may simply be the roles I play in various social niches, with self just a name for this apparent unity. Third, my apparent unity may be just various

168

stages which change as we age. Regarding this last argument, Flanagan concedes that there is no same self continuing over time, but that this does not show there is no self, just that it changes over time. Even granting the second argument that I am a social construction; I am still something, so the death of self does not follow. The first argument suggests determinism; but even if I am determined, I am still an agent who does things. So these death-of-subject arguments, while deflating our view of self, do not destroy it. Flanagan agrees that humans are contingent and do not posses eternal souls—but this does not mean they are not subjects.

But why is there anything at all? And why am I one of the things that is? Such questions invite answers such as: 1) the gods decided that the universe and creatures should exist and I have the chance to join them if I follow their commands; or 2) we don't know why there is anything except to say that the big bang and subsequent cosmic and biological evolution led to me. Flanagan notes that neither answer is satisfactory, because both posit something eternal—gods or physical facts. But that does not answer why there is something rather than nothing. (Reminiscent of earlier claims that we can't answer ultimate why questions.)

And yet many find the first story comforting, presumably because it links us with transcendent meaning. The second story has less appeal to most since it raises questions about one's significance, moral objectivity, concept of self, and ultimate meaning. But is the first story really more comforting than the second? How do the gods' plans make my life meaningful? And if the gods are the origin of all things are they really good? Thus it does not seem that either the theological or scientific story about origins can ground meaning in our lives.

Thus Flanagan suggests that we look elsewhere for meaning. Perhaps a person's meaning comes from relationships with others, or with work, or from nature—from things we can relate to in this life. After all, the scientific story never says that life does not matter. In fact a lot of things matter to me, from mundane things that I love to do—hiking and travel—to more long term projects that matter even more—learning, loving, and working creatively. This means that we are creatures that thrive on self-expression and, to the extent that we are not thwarted in this desire, can ameliorate the human condition and diminish the tragedy of our demise by this expression. As Flanagan concludes:

This is a kind of naturalistic transcendence, a way each of us, if we are lucky, can leave good-making traces beyond the time between our birth and death. To believe this sort of transcendence is possible is, I guess, to have a kind of religion. It involves believing that there are selves, that we can in self-expression make a difference, and if we use our truth detectors and good detectors well, that difference might be positive, a contribution to the cosmos.

Summary – We find meaning through self expression in our work and in our relationships.

Frankl: The Search for Meaning

Viktor Emil Frankl M.D., PhD. (1905 - 1997) was an Austrian neurologist and psychiatrist as well as a Holocaust survivor. Frankl was the founder of logo-therapy, a form of Existential Analysis, and best-selling book author of, *Man's Search For Meaning*, which belongs on any list of the most influential books in last half-century. It has sold over 12 million copies.

The first part of the book tells the story of his life in the concentration camps—needless to say it is not for the faint of heart. Although Frankl survived, his parents, brother, and pregnant wife all perished. (There is no good substitute for a close reading of the book to convey the unrelenting misery of the situation, or to appreciate Frankl's reflections on it.) The record of his personal experience and observation is a priceless cultural legacy.

Frankl's philosophical views that emanate from his experience begin with his quoting Nietzsche: "He who has a why to live can bear with almost any how." If we live to return to our loved ones or to finish our book, if we have a why to live for, if we have a meaning to live for, then we have a reason to survive, no matter how miserable the conditions of our lives. This desire to live, what Frankl calls "the will to meaning," is the primary motive of human life. Putting these ideas together we are driven by the desires to survive, exist, and find meaning.

Frankl believes that a large part of meaning is subjective. It is not what we expect from life but what it expects from us that will provide meaning. We are free and we are responsible for how we live our lives. In this way Frankl sounds like an existentialist and subjectivist, extolling us to create our own meaning. But we classify him as an objectivist, for in the end there are objective values, there are things in this world that can provide meaning for anyone. The three objective sources of meaning are: 1) the experience of goodness or beauty, or of loving others; 2) creative deeds or work; and 3) the attitude we take toward unavoidable suffering. It is easy to see that love or work could give life meaning. If others whom we love depend upon us, or if we have some noble work to finish, we have a meaning for our lives; we have a why for which to bear any how.

But how is the attitude we take toward suffering a potential source of meaning? Frankl says first that we reveal our inner freedom in the attitude we take toward unavoidable suffering; and secondly, like the Stoics, we can see our suffering as our task that we can bear nobly. Thus our suffering can be an achievement in which tragedy has been transformed into triumph. Frankl observed that prisoners who changed their attitudes toward suffering in this way were the ones who had the best chance of surviving. In the end Frankl makes a case for tragic optimism. Life may be tragic, but we should remain optimistic that it meaningful nonetheless— life even in its most tragic manifestations provides ways to make life meaningful.

Summary – Meaning in life is found in productive work, loving relationships, and enduring suffering nobly.

Meaning Found in Living: Tennyson, Kazantzakis, Durant

Tennyson: The Struggles of Ulysses

Maybe the key is not in our answers, but in our struggles. This is a salient theme in Homer's epic poem The Odyssey, which tells the story of Odysseus, the king of Ithaca, and his ten year journey home after the end of the ten year long Trojan War. Odysseus' tribulations on his homeward journey are legendary, as he battles giants, monsters, storms, and the sirens of beautiful women who call sailors to their death. After finally reaching home, reunited with his wife and his kingdom, Homer suggests that Odysseus desired to leave again, an idea picked up centuries later by Dante.

In the nineteenth century Alfred Lord Tennyson (1809 – 1892) expanded on this theme. Tennyson was the Poet Laureate of the United Kingdom during much of Queen Victoria's reign, and one of the most popular poets in the English language. His poem Ulysses, Odysseus' name in Latin, famously captured Ulysses' dissatisfaction with life in Ithaca after his return, and his subsequent desire to set sail again. Perhaps nothing in Western literature conveys the feeling of going forward and braving the struggle of life more movingly than this poem.

Who Are We?

Tennyson begins by describing the boredom and restlessness Ulysses experiences after finally returning to rule his kingdom.

> It little profits that an idle king,
> By this still hearth, among these barren crags,
> Matched with an aged wife, I mete and dole
> Unequal laws unto a savage race,
> That hoard, and sleep, and feed, and know not me.

Contrast these sentiments with his excitement that his memories elicit.

> I cannot rest from travel: I will drink
> Life to the lees: all times I have enjoyed
> Greatly, have suffered greatly, both with those
> That loved me, and alone; on shore, and when
> Through scudding drifts the rainy Hyades
> Vexed the dim sea: I am become a name;
> For always roaming with a hungry heart
> Much have I seen and known; cities of men
> And manners, climates, councils, governments,
> Myself not least, but honoured of them all;
> And drunk delight of battle with my peers;
> Far on the ringing plains of windy Troy.

He's nostalgic about his past, but he also longs for new experiences. He describes his restlessness perfectly:

> I am a part of all that I have met;
> Yet all experience is an arch wherethrough
> Gleams that untravelled world, whose margin fades
> For ever and for ever when I move.
> How dull it is to pause, to make an end,

> To rust unburnished, not to shine in use!
> As though to breathe were life.

Looking toward the sea with a restless heart, he again feels its pull.

> There lies the port; the vessel puffs her sail:
> There gloom the dark broad seas. My mariners,
> Souls that have toiled, and wrought, and thought
> with me—
> That ever with a frolic welcome took
> The thunder and the sunshine, and opposed
> Free hearts, free foreheads—you and I are old;
> Old age hath yet his honour and his toil;
> Death closes all: but something ere the end,
> Some work of noble note, may yet be done,
> Not unbecoming men that strove with Gods.

Finally, he gathers his fellow sailors and pushes out of the harbor for new adventures. Tennyson describes the scene and the sentiment with some of the greatest lines in the English language.

> The lights begin to twinkle from the rocks:
> The long day wanes: the slow moon climbs: the deep
> Moans round with many voices. Come, my friends,
> 'Tis not too late to seek a newer world.
> Push off, and sitting well in order smite
> The sounding furrows; for my purpose holds
> To sail beyond the sunset, and the baths
> Of all the western stars, until I die.
> It may be that the gulfs will wash us down:
> It may be we shall touch the Happy Isles,
> And see the great Achilles, whom we knew

Though much is taken, much abides; and though
We are not now that strength which in old days
Moved earth and heaven; that which we are, we are;
One equal temper of heroic hearts,
Made weak by time and fate, but strong in will
To strive, to seek, to find, and not to yield.

Ulysses found joy and meaning, not in port, but in his journeys, in the dark troubled sea of life which tosses us as we wrestle against it. There we find the thrill and the meaning of our lives as we battle without hope of ever finding a home. For Ulysses, the struggle was the meaning.

Kazantzakis: A Rejection of Hope

The power of the story of Ulysses was picked up by the famous Greek novelist Nikos Kazantzakis (1883 – 1957), who wrote a 33,333 line sequel to Homer's poem. In it the bored Ulysses gathers his followers, builds a boat, and sails away on a final journey, eventually dying in the Antarctic. According to Kazantzakis, Ulysses does not find what he's seeking, but it doesn't matter. Through the search itself he is ennobled—and the meaning of his life was found in the search. In the end his Ulysses cry out "My soul, your voyages have been your native land."

Perhaps no one thought deeper about longings, hope, and the meaning of life than Kazantzakis. In his early years he was particularly impressed with Nietzsche's Dionysian vision of humans shaping themselves into the superman, and with Bergson's idea of the elan vital. From Nietzsche he learned that by sheer force of will humans can be free as long as they proceed without fear or hope of reward. From Bergson, under whom he studied in Paris, he came to believe that a vital evolutionary life force molds matter, potentially creating higher forms of life. Putting these ideas together, Kazantzakis declared that we find the meaning of life by struggling against universal entropy, an idea he connected with god. For Kazantzakis the word god referred to "the anti-entropic life-force that organizes elemental matter into systems that can manifest ever more subtle and advanced forms of beings and consciousness." The meaning of our lives is to find our place in the chain that links us with these undreamt of forms of life.

> We all ascend together, swept up by a mysterious and invisible urge. Where are we going? No one knows. Don't ask, mount higher! Perhaps we are going nowhere, perhaps there is no one to pay us the rewarding wages of our lives. So much the better! For thus may we conquer the last, the greatest of all temptations—that of Hope.

The honest and brave struggle without hope or expectation that they will ever arrive, ever be anchored, ever be at home. Like Ulysses, the only home Kazantzakis found was in the search itself. The meaning of life is found in the search and the struggle.

In the prologue of his autobiography, Report to Greco, Kazantzakis claims that we need to go beyond both hope and despair. Both expectation of paradise and fear of hell prevent us from focusing on what is in front of us, our heart's true homeland … the search for meaning itself. We ought to be warriors who struggle bravely to create meaning without expecting anything in return. Unafraid of the abyss, we should face it bravely and run toward it. Ultimately we find joy by taking full responsibility for our lives— joyous in the face of tragedy. Life is essentially struggle, and if in the end it judges us we should bravely reply:

> General, the battle draws to a close and I make my report. This is where and how I fought. I fell wounded, lost heart, but did not desert. Though my teeth clattered from fear, I

bound my forehead tightly with a red handkerchief to hide the blood, and ran to the assault.

Surely that is as courageous a sentiment in response to the ordeal of human life as has been offered in world literature. It is a bold rejoinder to the awareness of the inevitable decline of our minds and bodies, as well as to the existential agonies that permeate life. It finds the meaning of life in our actions, our struggles, our battles, our roaming, our wandering, and our journeying. It appeals to nothing other than what we know and experience—and yet finds meaning and contentment there.

Just outside the city walls of Heraklion Crete one can visit Kazantzakis' gravesite, located there as the Orthodox Church denied his being buried in a Christian cemetery. On the black, jagged, cracked, unpolished Cretan marble you will find no name to designate who lies there, no dates of birth or death, only an epitaph in Greek carved in the stone. It translates: "I hope for nothing. I fear nothing. I am free."

Durant: Finding Meaning in Everything

Will Durant, one of the most popular historians and prose stylists of the twentieth-century, wondered if there is something suggestive about the cycle of a human life which sheds light on meaning, a theme explored in his 1929 book *The Mansions of Philosophy*. He grants that "life is in its basis a mystery, a river flowing from an unseen source; and in its development an infinite subtlety too complex for thought, much less for utterance." Yet we seek answers nonetheless. Undeterred by the difficulty of his task, Durant suggests that reflection on the microcosm of a human life might yield insights about the meaning of all life and death. Thus he looks at a typical human life cycle for clues about cosmic meaning.

Chapter 6 – The Meaning of Life

In children Durant saw curiosity, growth, urgency, playfulness, and discontent. In later youth the struggle continues as we learn to read, work, love, and learn of the world's evils. In middle age we are often consumed by work and family life, and for the first time we see the reality of death. Still, in family life people usually find great pleasure, and the best of all human conditions.

In old age the reality of death comes nearer. If we have lived well we might graciously leave the stage for better players to perform a better play. But what if life endlessly repeats its sufferings, with youth making the same mistakes as their elders, and all leading to death? Is this the final realization of old age? Such thoughts gnaw at our heart and poison aging.

So Durant wonders if we must die for life. If we are not individuals but cells in life's body, then we die so that life remains strong, death removing the rubbish as the new life created defeats death. This perpetuation of life gives life meaning. "If it is one test of philosophy to give life a meaning that shall frustrate death, wisdom will show that corruption comes only to the part, that life itself is deathless while we die." So the individual dies, but life goes on endlessly forward. On their deathbeds the aged speak to the harsh winter that is life, death seems to win; outside, children speak to the hopeful spring, life wins.

Still we remain forlorn. Perhaps we should give up our ego attachment, and leave for the sake of the species. But why? What's wrong with loving life so much that one never wants to let go? Besides it is wasteful for life to start over each time, having to relearn old truths and unlearn old falsehoods. As for life winning, it may instead destroy itself, and even if it doesn't we will not survive as individuals. In the end nothing in Durant's portrait soothes our worries about the futility of an infinite repetition.

178

Who Are We?

In 1930 Durant received a number of letters from persons declaring their intent to commit suicide. They asked Durant, by that time a popular public intellectual, for reasons to go on living. In his book *On the Meaning of Life* (1932) Durant tried to answer their queries by extending the theme found in Tennyson, Kazantzakis, and Maurois. He suggests that we cannot answer the question in any absolute sense, for our minds are too small to comprehend things in their entirety. Nonetheless he does believe we can say a few things about terrestrial meaning:

> The meaning of life, then, must lie within itself ... it must be sought in life's own instinctive cravings and natural fulfillments. Why, for example, should we ask for an ulterior meaning to vitality and health? ... If you are sick beyond cure I will grant you viaticum, and let you die ... But if you are well—if you can stand on your legs and digest your food—forget your whining, and shout your gratitude to the sun.

> The simplest meaning of life then is joy—the exhilaration of experience itself, of physical well-being ... If the child is happier than the man it is because it has more body and less soul, and understands that nature comes before philosophy; it asks for no further meaning to its arms and legs than their abounding use ...

We should be particularly thankful for our fellows; they are a primary reason for loving life.

> Do not be so ungrateful about love ... to the attachment of friends and mates who have gone hand in hand through much hell, some purgatory, and a little heaven, and have been soldered into unity by being burned together in the

179

flame of life. I know such mates or comrades quarrel regularly, and get upon each other's nerves; but there is ample recompense for that in the unconscious consciousness that someone is interested in you, depends upon you, exaggerates you, and is waiting to meet you at the station. Solitude is worse than war.

Love relates the individual to something more than itself, to some whole which gives it purpose.

I note that those who are cooperating parts of a whole do not despond; the despised "yokel" playing ball with his fellows in the lot is happier than these isolated thinkers, who stand aside from the game of life and degenerate through the separation … If we think of ourselves as part of a living … group, we shall find life a little fuller … For to give life a meaning one must have a purpose larger and more enduring than one's self … ask the father of sons and daughters "What is the meaning of life?" and he will answer you very simply: "Feeding our family."

Durant too finds meaning in love, connection, and activity. "The secret of significance and content is to have a task which consumes all one's energies, and makes human life a little richer than before." Durant found the most happiness in his family and his work, in his home and his books. Although no one can be fully happy amidst poverty and suffering, one can be content and grateful finding the meaning in front of them. "Where, in the last resort, does my treasure lie?—in everything."

Cosmic Evolution and the Meaning of Life

A study of cosmic evolution can support the claim that life has become increasingly meaningful, a claim buttressed primarily by the emergence of beings with conscious purposes and meanings. Where there once was no meaning or purpose—in a universe without mind—there is now both meanings and purposes. These meanings have their origin in the matter which coalesced into stars and planets, which in turn supported organisms that evolved bodies with brains and their attributes—behavior, consciousness, personal identity, freedom, value, and meaning. Meaning has emerged during the evolutionary process. It came into being when complexly organized brains, consisting of constitutive parts and the interactive relationships between those parts, intermingled with physical and then cultural environments. This relationship was reciprocal—brains affected biological and cognitive environments which in turn affected those brains. The result of this interaction between organisms and environments was a reality that became, among other things, infused with meaning.

But will meaning continue to emerge as evolution moves forward? Will progressive evolutionary trends persevere to complete or final meaning, or to approaching meaning as a limit? Will the momentum of cognitive development make such progress nearly inevitable? These are different questions—ones which we cannot answer confidently. We could construct an inductive argument, that the past will resemble the future in this regard, but such an argument is not convincing. For who knows what will happen in the future? The human species might bring about its own ruin tomorrow or go extinct due to some biological, geophysical, or astronomical phenomenon. We cannot bridge the gap between what has happened and what will happen. The future is unknown.

All this leads naturally to another question. Is the emergence of meaning a good thing? It is easy enough to say that conscious beings create meaning, but it is altogether different to say that this is a positive development. Before consciousness no one derived meaning from torturing others, but now they sometimes do. In this case a new kind of meaning emerged, but few think this is a plus. Although we can establish the emergence of meaning, we cannot establish that this is good.

Still, we fantasize that our scientific knowledge will improve both the quality and quantity of life. We will make ourselves immortal, build ourselves better brains, and transform our moral natures—making life better and more meaningful, perhaps fully meaningful. We will become pilots worthy of steering evolution to fantastic heights, toward creating a heaven on earth or in simulated realities of our design. If meaning and value continue to emerge we will find meaning by partaking in, and hastening along, that very process. As the result of past meanings and as the conduit for the emergence of future ones, we could be the protagonists of a great epic that ascends higher.

In our imagination we exist as links in a golden chain leading onward and upward toward greater levels of being, consciousness, joy, beauty, goodness, and meaning—perhaps even to their apex. As part of such a glorious process we find meaning instilled into our lives from previously created meaning, and we reciprocate by emanating meaning back into a universe with which we are ultimately one. Evolutionary thought, extended beyond its normal bounds, is an extraordinarily speculative, quasi-religious metaphysics in which a naturalistic heaven appears on the horizon.

Yet, as we ascend these mountains of thought, we are brought back to earth. When we look to the past we see that evolution has produced meaning, but it has also produced pain, fear, genocide, extinction, war, loneliness, anguish, envy, slavery, despair, futility, torture, guilt, depression, alienation, ignorance, torture, inequality, superstition, poverty, heartache, death, and meaninglessness. Surely serious reflection on this misery is sobering. Turning to the future, our optimism must be similarly restrained. Fantasies about

182

where evolution is headed should be tempered, if for no other reason than that our increased powers can be used for evil as well as for our improvement. Our wishes may never be fulfilled.

But this is not all. It is not merely that we cannot know if our splendid speculations are true—which we cannot—it is that we have an overwhelmingly strong reason to reject our flights of fancy. And that is that humans are notorious pattern-seekers, story-tellers, and meaning-makers who invariably weave narratives around these patterns and stories to give meaning to their lives. It follows that the patterns of progress we glimpse likely exist only in our minds. There is no face of a man on Mars or of Jesus on grilled cheese sandwiches. If we find patterns of progress in evolution, we are probably victims of simple confirmation bias.

After all progress is hardly the whole story of evolution, as most species and cultures have gone extinct, a fate that may soon befall us. Furthermore, as this immense universe (or multi-verse) is largely incomprehensible to us, with our three and a half pound brains, we should hesitate to substitute an evolutionary-like religion for our frustrated metaphysical longings. We should be more reticent about advancing cosmic visions, and less credulous about believing in them. Our humility should temper our grandiose metaphysical speculations. In short, if reflection on a scientific theory supposedly reveals that our deepest wishes are true, our skeptical alarm bell should go off. We need to be braver than that, for we want to know, not just to believe. In our job as serious seekers of the truth, the credulous need not apply.

Thus we cannot confidently answer all of the questions we posed at the beginning of this essay in the affirmative. We can say that there has been some progress in evolution and that meaning has emerged in the process, but we cannot say these trends will continue or that they were good. And we certainly must guard

183

against speculative metaphysical fantasies, inasmuch as there are good reasons to think we are not special. We don't know that a meaningful eschatology will gradually unfold as we evolve, much less that we could articulate a cosmic vision to describe it. We don't even know if the reality of any grand cosmic vision is possible. We are moving, but we might be moving toward our own extinction, toward universal death, or toward eternal hell. And none of those offer much comfort.

We long to dream but always our skepticism awakens us from our Pollyannaish imaginings. The evolution of the cosmos, our species, and our intelligence gives us some grounds for believing that life might become more meaningful, but not enough to satisfy our longings. For we want to believe that tomorrow will really be better than yesterday. We want to believe that a glorious future awaits but, detached from our romanticism, we know there may be no salvation; there may be no comfort to be found for our harassed souls.

Confronted with such meager prospects and the anguish that accompanies them, we are lost, and the most we can do, once again, is hope. That doesn't give us what we want or need, but it does give us something we don't have to be ashamed of. There is nothing irrational about the kind of hope that is elicited by, and best expressed from, an evolutionary perspective. Julian Huxley, scientist and poet, best conveyed these hopes:

> I turn the handle and the story starts:
> Reel after reel is all astronomy,
> Till life, enkindled in a niche of sky,
> Leaps on the stage to play a million parts.
>
> Life leaves the slime and through the oceans darts;
> She conquers earth, and raises wings to fly;

Then spirit blooms, and learns how not to die,
Nesting beyond the grave in others' hearts.

I turn the handle; other men like me
Have made the film; and now I sit and look
In quiet, privileged like Divinity
To read the roaring world as in a book.
If this thy past, where shall thy future climb,
O Spirit, built of Elements and Time!

The Meaning of Life

Uncertain that life will ever be completely meaningful, or that we will participate in such meaning if even it does come to pass, we can still hope that our lives are significant, that our descendants will live more meaningful lives than we do, that our science and technology will save us, and that life will culminate in, or at least approach, complete meaning. These hopes help us to brave the struggle of life, keeping alive the possibility that we will create a better and more meaningful reality. Hope is useful.

The possibility of infinitely long, good, and meaningful lives brings the purpose of our lives into focus. *The purpose of life is to diminish and, if possible, abolish all constraints on our being— intellectual, psychological, physical, and moral—and remake the external world in ways conducive to the emergence of meaning.* This implies embracing our role as protagonists of the cosmic evolutionary epic, working to increase the quantity and quality of knowledge, love, joy, pleasure, beauty, goodness and meaning in the world, while diminishing their opposites. This is the purpose of our lives.

In a concrete way this implies being better thinkers, friends, lovers, artists, and parents. It means caring for the planet that sustains us and acting in ways that promote the flourishing of all

185

being. Naturally there are disagreements about what this entails and how we move from theory to practice, but the way forward should become increasing clear as we achieve higher states of being and consciousness. As we become more intellectually and morally virtuous.

Nonetheless, knowing the purpose of our lives doesn't ensure that they are fully meaningful, for we may collectively fail in our mission to give life more meaning; we may not achieve our purpose. And if we don't fulfill our purpose, then life wasn't fully meaningful. Thus the tentative answer to our question—is life ultimately meaningful—is that we know how life could be ultimately meaningful, but we don't know if it is or will be ultimately meaningful. Life can be judged fully meaningful from an eternal perspective only if we fulfill our purpose by making it better and more meaningful.

Meaning then, like the consciousness and freedom from which it derives, is an emergent property of cosmic evolution—and we find our purpose by playing our small part in aiding its emergence. If we are successful our efforts will culminate in the overcoming of human limitations, and our (post-human) descendents will live fully meaningful lives. If we do achieve our purpose in the far distant future, if a fully meaningful reality comes to fruition, and if somehow we are a part of that meaningful reality, then we could say that our life and all life was, and is, deeply meaningful. In the interim we can find inspiration—we can find meaning in life—in the hope that we can succeed.

Final Thoughts

We end with some words from Bertrand Russell, perhaps the greatest philosopher of the twentieth-century. Russell made a number of attempts to sum up the meaning of life. We've seen one

of them already in his essay "A Free Man's Worship." Another
was written in his eighties as the introduction to his autobiography.
It is may be the most moving and profound piece of short prose
I've ever read.

> Three passions, simple but overwhelmingly strong, have
> governed my life: the longing for love, the search for
> knowledge, and unbearable pity for the suffering of
> mankind. These passions, like great winds, have blown me
> hither and thither, in a wayward course, over a great ocean
> of anguish, reaching to the very verge of despair.
>
> I have sought love, first, because it brings ecstasy—ecstasy
> so great that I would often have sacrificed all the rest of life
> for a few hours of this joy. I have sought it, next, because it
> relieves loneliness—that terrible loneliness in which one
> shivering consciousness looks over the rim of the world
> into the cold unfathomable lifeless abyss. I have sought it
> finally, because in the union of love I have seen, in a mystic
> miniature, the prefiguring vision of the heaven that saints
> and poets have imagined. This is what I sought, and though
> it might seem too good for human life, this is what—at
> last—I have found.
>
> With equal passion I have sought knowledge. I have wished
> to understand the hearts of men. I have wished to know
> why the stars shine. And I have tried to apprehend the
> Pythagorean power by which number holds sway above the
> flux. A little of this, but not much, I have achieved.
>
> Love and knowledge, so far as they were possible, led
> upward toward the heavens. But always pity brought me
> back to earth. Echoes of cries of pain reverberate in my

heart. Children in famine, victims tortured by oppressors, helpless old people a burden to their sons, and the whole world of loneliness, poverty, and pain make a mockery of what human life should be. I long to alleviate this evil, but I cannot, and I too suffer.

Russell's last surviving manuscript was unknown to anyone until a Russell archivist saw a copy in a book of photographs published to mark Russell's centenary in 1972. One of the pictures was of Russell's study in north Wales and on his desk was a manuscript dated 1967. Shortly before her death Russell's wife Edith handed it over to the archives. The manuscript was not made public until 1993, on the 25th anniversary of the opening of the archives.

In it Russell made one final attempt to summarize his thoughts about life's meaning. At that time it was written Russell was 95 years old, and rumored to be senile or at least no longer capable of coherent writing. The hand written page proved otherwise, displaying a lucidity of style that eludes most writers at their peak.

It began: "The time has come to review my life as a whole, and to ask whether it has served any useful purpose or has been wholly concerned in futility. Unfortunately, no answer is possible for anyone who does not know the future." After so many years of study, an answer to the most important question we can ask was not forthcoming. Yet a glimmer of optimism remained. The final sentences ever written from the pen of one of Western civilizations great writers and philosophers looked—as we have—to the future.

Consider for a moment what our planet is and what it might be. At present, for most, there is toil and hunger, constant danger, more hatred than love. There could be a happy world, where co-operation was more in evidence than competition, and monotonous work is done by machines, where what is lovely in nature is not destroyed to make room for hideous machines whose sole business is to kill, and where to promote joy is more respected than to produce mountains of corpses. Do not say this is impossible: it is not. It waits only for men to desire it more than the infliction of torture.

There is an artist imprisoned in each one of us. Let him loose to spread joy everywhere.

Made in the USA
San Bernardino, CA
20 March 2017